DIGITAL MARKETING FOR EVERYONE

Christos Visvardis

Christos Visvardis has worked for Facebook and other tech companies. He helps businesses optimize their performance and improve their decision making. You can contact him for your business problems at *christos@visvardis.com*

CONTENTS

THE FOUNDATIONS

A brave new digital world

Going online these days is not just a trend; it uncovers a whole new world of opportunities for your business.

By going online, you can find new customers, since more than half of the world's population have access to the Internet and more than 2 billion people own a smartphone.

You don't need to rely on a physical store; you can sell your products directly from your e-shop. You can target specific audiences and deliver related ads, as well as get info on what your users are interested in. Moreover, you can use the power of data and analytics to get actionable insights and make better decisions.

All the above can be applied to any type and size of business (the book is called Digital Marketing for Everyone after all!) but let's see an example of a small business harnessing the power of the online world.

Let's say you own a beauty salon. So far, your business has grown through word of mouth in the local community thanks to the great work you've been doing. You don't have a digital presence, but you'd like to grow your business. Is going online worth it for you?

The first benefit you will get by being online is that people can search for your business on search engines like Google, Bing etc. When someone wants to find a beauty salon in their town they will Google something like "beauty salon near me" and your shop will appear in the search results.

What's in it for you, you say? When someone clicks to the search result for your beauty salon they're directed to your website where they learn about your business and get acquainted with your brand. You can have a video showcasing all the different beauty services you offer, the website visitors can read testimonials from happy customers, look at your pricelist, find your contact details and map directions, learn about your offers.

Maybe they'll take it a step further and ill in an online form with their info so you can contact them back about a question or they can even book a session. They might click on your social media links and follow you on Facebook, Instagram, Twitter where they can regularly read your updates, see your photos and have a conversation with you.

Not everything on the above example might be applicable to your business or you might want to start only with a few of the above features, but you should understand that the possibilities are virtually endless.

And we haven't even mentioned everything! The power of data should not be underestimated. Your website or app gives you insights on your customer behaviors: what they like and what works for your business.

You can target people who fit the profile of what your business offers, or you can find people interested in your services.

For example, search advertising allows you to show your ads to people searching for terms relevant to your business. You might want to show the ads to people who live in your area only and you can use analytics tools to find out if people clicked on your ads (or which ad brings back the best results) or what they do on your website (e.g. which page do they spend most time on?).

What is more, most of the tools and features mentioned above can be learned and used easily (like in this book!) and you can have free access to many of them.

In fact, it's not the tools you should really worry about, but your digital plan. It's all about the business after all! The tools are just there to help you, just like this very book you're reading right now.

You should start by considering what you want to do and where to start from. Do you want a web presence (website), mobile (app or mobile website), social media (Facebook, Instagram, Snapchat, Twitter etc.) or all of them?

Are you going to deal with the content, creative and technical part of your digital strategy? Do you have the time to learn the tools and maintain your digital presence or are you going to pay a specialist or digital agency to help you with it? There is no right answer for this, but you have to consider the tradeoffs?

If you're just starting with a small business and its online presence, I suggest you learn the ropes and start doing things yourself. If you find that you don't have the time, then you can delegate the work to someone externally or even hire a person to do this for you in-house.

Also, set your goals, budget and schedule. What do you want to achieve and what will this cost in time and money?

The time to go online and it couldn't be better. The technology, know-how and tools are at your disposal so you can take your business to the next level.

Setting your goals

Any plan should start with your goals and your goals should align with your business objective. Know what you'd like to achieve online and set priorities.

The first question you should ask yourself is why. If you have a beauty salon as we already used as an example, your business goal is to sell more of your services (facial cleanings, manicure, pedicure etc.) and also sell more of the beauty products that you offer in-store.

In order to get people to buy your services, they have to know your beauty salon first. This is something that can be achieved through digital marketing.

So, in our example, let's start with spreading the word for your business as your first digital goal.

First, you can list your business in online directories, so when people search for beauty salons, they can come across your business.

You can also build a website to provide more info to your potential customers (contact details, pricelist, services, photos, videos) and set up your social media profiles/pages on Facebook, Snapchat, Instagram to post highly engaging photos of satisfied customers, showcase your services and your offers.

More people will start following your business and then you might reach a point where your goal actually evolves into getting people who follow you to become paying customers instead of just generating exposure and awareness for your business.

Based on those new goals you could work on digital features like booking an appointment through your website, online reviews, and an online shop to sell your beauty products.

After getting visitors to your website and social media pages you can use paid advertising to expand your business.

What is more, you need to be measuring your digital activities. The term analytics is the umbrella term for this and can be used to show what works and what you can improve.

Laying the foundations

In the movie Field of Dreams, Kevin Costner builds a baseball diamond after hearing a voice telling him "If you build it, he will come." In digital marketing, building your presence does not ensure people will come to it, but you sure have to build something first.

Your options include websites, mobile apps, social media etc. and it's actually really easy to build them.

It used to be the case that a website should be the first step that you take towards your digital presence, but you don't necessarily need to start there nowadays.

In the beauty salon example, you can start by listing your business in online directories (e.g. Google My Business) or create a social media page.

When someone searches for beauty salons in your area, they'll see your business in search results.

And by visiting your Facebook page they could get more info on your business. In either case, no website is required.

Moreover, both a Facebook page and a listing on Google My Business are totally free. Whereas a website will probably have some costs like buying a domain name, hosting and even paying someone to design your website. Although, these costs are relatively small you can still start with just the totally free options you have on social media and online listings.

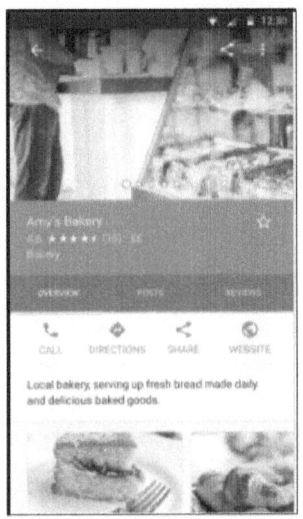

An example of a Google My Business entry.

At some point, however, you will want to build a website, as this will be your online storefront. Once again, what is important is that you know what you want to achieve with it. How are people going to use it?

Do you want them to call you? Make sure your phone number is prominent on the homepage.

Or you might want them to find your actual shop? Then make sure there is a map and directions on the website.

Maybe, you'd like to have people book appointments. Then, you can build an online form for this.

Or you might want to sell products from you online. You'll have to include an e-shop on your website where people can order beauty products and make payments online.

With mobile being the king in digital nowadays, many companies choose to also create mobile apps for their customers.

Apps can be useful for creating loyalty programs, sending notifications etc.

We'll see all the above options in more details, but also find out how you can get more people to see what you've built.

You built it, but how are they going to come?

And now that you've built your online home, you need to bring some guests to it, right? Let's see how you can utilize digital marketing to attract customers.

You have a few different digital options, as you might have guessed. First of all, search engines (Google, Bing etc.). People use search engines to find specific answers for their requests. This is really powerful because users know exactly what they're looking for on a search engine, thus making search users more likely to buy services and products relevant to their searches.

Search engines will show your business in their results for relevant services. There are two ways to show up on search engine results. The first one is Search Engine Optimization (SEO), which is free and helps you promote your business in the unpaid (also known as organic) search results.

The second is Search Engine Marketing (SEM), i.e. buying ad space in the search results. You might be asking why should you buy ads when you can feature in search results for free? The reason is that ads show up in the top results of a search page and, considering all the similar pages and businesses competing for the same search results, it pays off to buy the right ads.

The foundation of SEO is keywords – what people type in the search engine. These are the most relevant terms for your business, e.g. for a beauty salon it would be keywords like "facial cleaning", "massage", "manicure", "beauty salon" etc.

Knowing what keywords people use will help improve your chances of showing up in organic search results. SEM is all about paying for specific keywords. Google and other search engines use an auction system, where multiple businesses will compete for the same keyword. Every business makes a bid for that keyword and the top ones will be shown as ads in the search results.

As we'll see later advertisers are ranked based on several factors – not just their bid.

Google search results for "car insurance" on a desktop computer. Note that the two first results are marked as ads (meaning they are paid or SEM results) whereas the rest of the search results are organic/SEO. As you can see paid results are always shown on top making them more likely to bring customers than organic results.

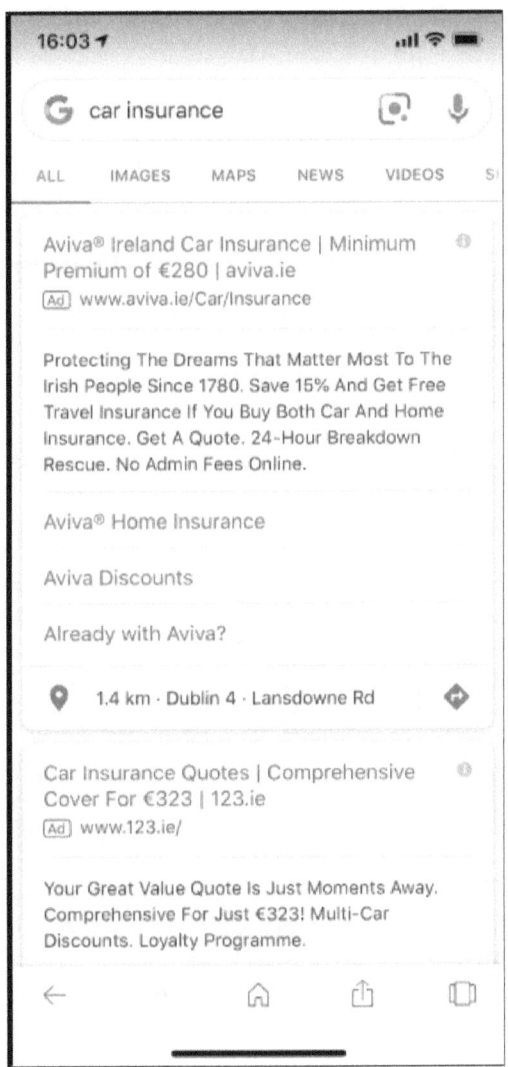

Google search results on a mobile device. Note that due to the screen size of mobile devices only two results (both paid as marked by the word "Ad" in green) are featured unless you scroll down. Since most people are on mobile these days this has to be taken into consideration when designing your search strategy.

Your digital marketing plan has to take into account how people use the web. Most people will browse different websites to read the news, watch videos, get informed on their favorite sports team and, in general, access a big and varied amount of content.

A lot of websites will show ads alongside this content which is referred to as "display advertising".

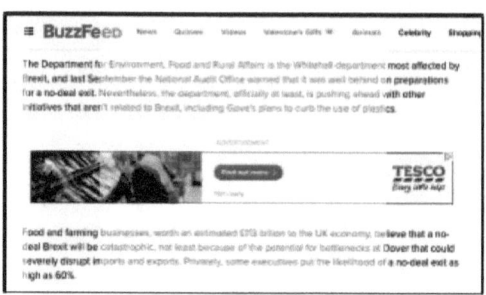

An example of a display ad (advertising Tesco and clearly marked as advertisement on top of the banner) on BuzzFeed.com.

Display ads are omnipresent nowadays and come in many different formats (static image, text, video etc.).

You can select the websites that your ad will appear on and target specific audiences that are relevant to your ad.

Another way to reach people is social media, like Facebook, Instagram, Twitter. Social media are a great way to build awareness for your business and cultivate relationships with your customers.

Start by creating a page or profile on the biggest social networks. Literally billions of people around the world use social media and they follow the people, organizations and companies that they find interesting.

You can post content and start conversations with your followers to boost your business' profile and awareness.

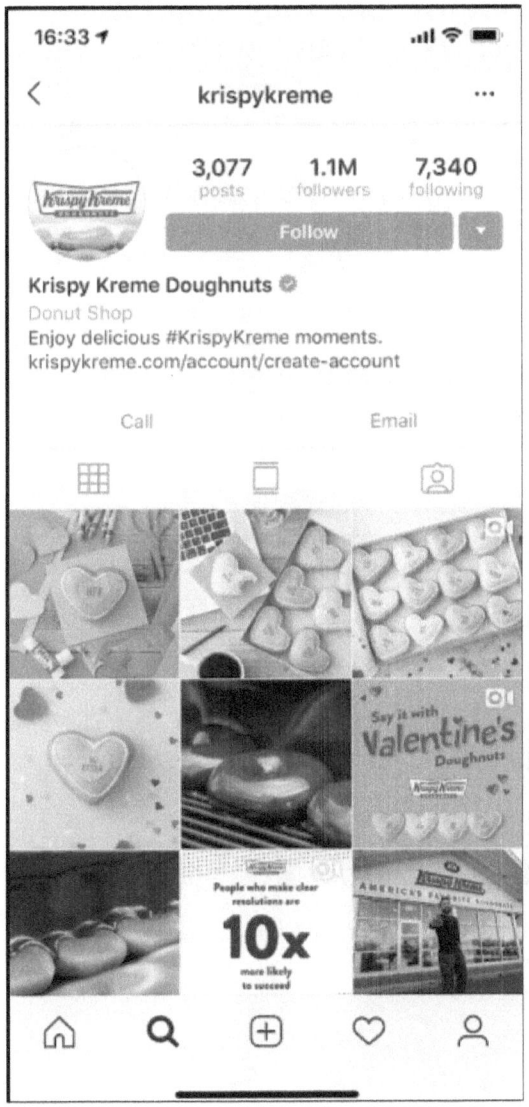

The Instagram page of Krispy Kreme which uses social media as a
big part of their digital marketing strategy.

Last but not least, email marketing has always been an efficient
and cost-effective way of reaching your audiences. Remember

that it is imperative that people opt-in to your newsletter; spamming is not OK and can actually have legal repercussions for your company. Moreover, spamming will ultimately back-fire, creating a bad reputation for your business.

What we're talking about here is sending valuable and relevant information or offers to people who have chosen to follow you through email.

Email communication is free but getting people to sign up for your newsletter might still require that you spend money on some paid ads so that people discover it. As soon as people sign up for this kind of communication you can send them vouchers or inform them about events and sales.

A newsletter by GameStop with weekly sales and promotions.

Keeping score

Your work doesn't end at building and marketing your online presence. You have to ensure that you're meeting the goals you set initially.

First, remember that it can take a while to set up your digital presence. Don't get disappointed, as it takes time for search engines to find your content and people to discover you on social media.

So, if you're starting to sell your products online, the sales for the first weeks or months will probably be low.

A significant part of your digital plan is to keep track of what you're doing. The umbrella term for this is "analytics", i.e. looking at your data to see what areas you can improve and if you're on track to meet your goals.

There's a lot of minutiae when it comes to analytics, but as a first step you'll probably want to see where your customers and online visitors come from to find your website. Did they see a display ad, or did they find you through social media? This way you know on what to spend your money and effort on.

Moreover, looking at your customers' behavior on your website (e.g. which pages they spend a lot of time on etc.) can help you figure out what they like and if their digital experience is valuable.

For example, if you see that a lot of people visit your website but not the page where you sell your products, you might have made it difficult for them to navigate to that part of the site. You want to design your website so that you direct people to take meaningful actions for your business.

Keep in mind that the digital world is constantly evolving. New tools, technologies and formats emerge every day. Your plan should be built on the basic concepts and foundations that don't change very much because they represent your business goals. But always keep an eye on the latest advancements and trends.

Moreover, make sure that the changes in your industry and business are reflected in your digital plan.

Wrapping up, your digital plan should be built on solid and realistic goals. Then you should us analytics to measure what you're doing and how it's performing. And finally, stay informed and up-to-date in order to adapt to the constant changes.

WEBSITES

Your web presence

The most common way to go digital is by creating a website. Nowadays, websites are not just online brochures but have interactive features which enable you to read reviews, watch videos, chat with customer help, buy products online and many more.

Once again, the website must align with your business goals. Technology is there to serve your business and not the other way around, so before you implement the new shiny format think if it actually makes sense for you and your customers.

As we mentioned before, you can have a perfectly adequate digital presence even without a website. In the case of a beauty salon, if someone searches for "pedicure" on Google, your listing shows up, they call you to arrange a visit and you just acquired a customer without a website.

As a matter of fact, if your website wouldn't have any further info and value than what the listing on Google includes it might be unnecessary or even counterproductive as it might add an extra step for your customer's online experience. Remember that a lot of users tend to abandon the online experience (or drop off as we say in digital marketing parlance) even if you add just an extra click or action that they have to take.

Digital should be about making things convenient for your customers – always remember that.

Moreover, people tend to visit websites like TripAdvisor, Foursquare or Yelp where they can see reviews about the type of places they're looking for. These reviews tend to be seen as more trusted than the reviews someone would find on your website. In many cases, reviews can make or break a business!

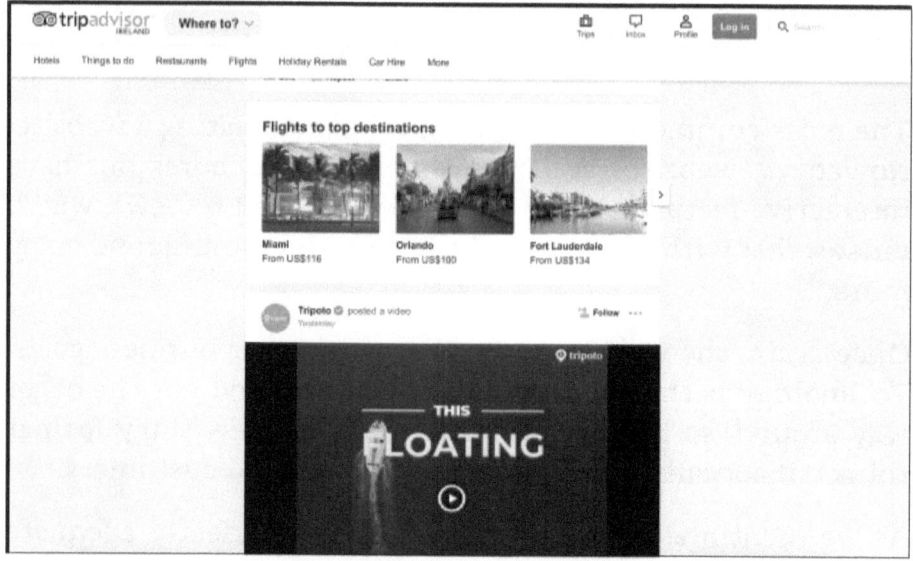

The popular review site TripAdvisor.

Moreover, people and business increasingly use social media to replace traditional websites. Most small businesses nowadays tend to start with a Facebook or Instagram page instead of a website, as they can reach literally billions of people with the same info that they would have on their website.

If mobile is really important for your business, you can even create an app which you can use to take advantage of features like GPS or enable people to order directly through your app.

If a user has your app, for example, you can send them a notification every time they are near your shop and inform them about a special offer. Or a user might use the app to pick up their order from your shop instead of waiting in line. And for repeat customers, a loyalty program through the app might give them an incentive to spend more money, more often and for a longer period.

All the above are options for your online presence and in the next few pages we'll focus on websites.

What is a website?

Without getting into all the technical minutiae, it's important to know how websites work.

A website can be your company's home on the Internet. It can serve as the first point of contact for your customers where people learn about your business.

In order to have a website you need to have space on server, i.e. a computer that hosts websites. There are loads of companies that offer this service and it can be as cheap as a few dollars per year to have your website hosted on a server.

The server is responsible for storing all the necessary components for your website (code, images etc.) and showing it to users when they type in your web address in their browser.

Every server in the world has an address, called an IP address. IP stands for Internet Protocol which is a set of rules on how websites and servers exchange information on the Internet.

An IP address consists of a series of digits, but fortunately we can choose easy-to-remember names that reference those numeric addresses.

This is usually called "domain name" and it's the way for people to find your website on the web. For example, nike.com is the domain name for the company Nike (and its corresponding IP address is 146.197.184.71; try typing this string of digits in your web browser and you should end up on www.nike.com).

Anything after the "www." part is your domain name and you should choose something that represents your business. For example, let's say you own a fashion company called "Amazing Dresses" and you've bought the domain amazingdresses.com.

Every time someone types this address on their browser, the

browser finds the server which holds the content for this website and "asks" the server to show that webpage.

The server "replies" by saying "I'm sending the code, 8 images and a video". The browser receives the info and puts it all together, ending up showing a nice webpage on your screen.

This is why IP is a communication protocol between computers, although instead of saying "hello" to each other they just send a series of bits and bytes.

The elements of a website

Let's start by choosing a domain name. That's what people will type into a browser (Chrome, Firefox, Safari etc.) to find your website.

First of all, you need to check if the domain is available. Every domain name is unique and if someone has already claimed it, you can't use it.

To know if a domain name is taken you can use any domain registrar or domain hosting service and when you search for a specific name you'll be informed if it's already claimed by someone else.

If a domain name is taken the registrar will suggest some alternatives; for example, if you search for beautysalon.com and it's already taken the service might suggest beatysalon.org or beauty-salon.com.

Companies usually use the extension .com for their websites, non-profits use .org and there's a two-letter domain name extension for every country (.fr for France, .jp for Japan etc.).

Make sure you choose a name that represents your business (ideally your brand or business name) and not some vague or unrelated domain. This will be important for search engines when showing results for searches related to your company's name.

A website usually consists of at least a home page and probably several other pages. The home page is the first page people see when they type in your domain name in a browser.

This is the equivalent to a shop window. Here's your chance to explain what you do and make it enticing for people to visit more of your pages or take a specific action (e.g. sign up for a newsletter or buy something).

A menu is usually one of the main components of a website which people can use to navigate to the main sections (e.g. e-shop, contact page etc.).

The way a site is planned is quite significant. Start from the user experience and try to get ideas from your favorite websites. How are they organized? The most successful online companies make it fast and easy to navigate around the site and take actions.

Take the online fashion retailer Asos for example. Like any clothes store that respects itself, asos.com will present you with two options on the homepage: women's or men's fashion. That's the first thing you would probably search for when entering a physical store as well.

Moreover, notice that the design of the homepage is uncluttered and only presents the info you need to know for your first action. Imagine if instead they showed you thousands of their different clothing options, which might be irrelevant to you. Not very helpful and inviting, right?

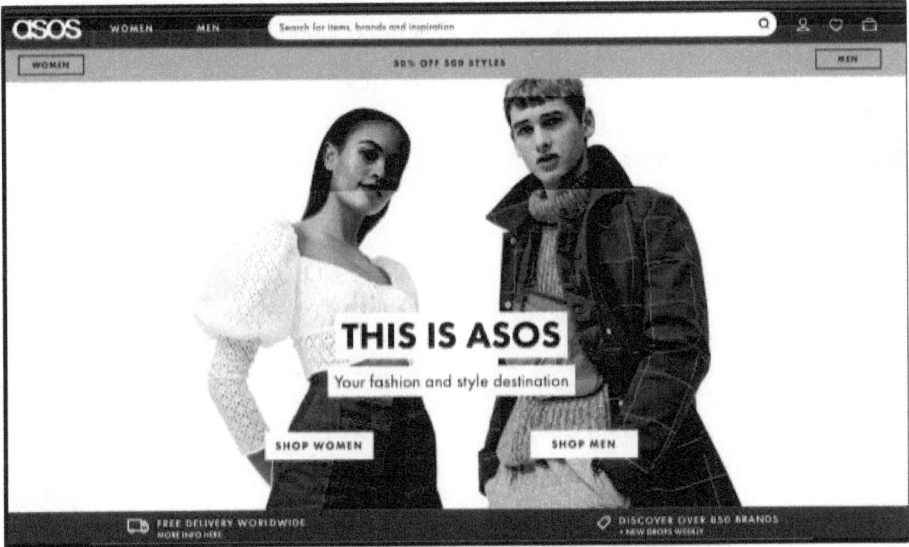

Asos.com homepage is uncluttered and presents you with two clear options, women's or men's fashion.

Next, decide what content you need to present on your website. You don't need to start from scratch: website building tools like WordPress offer templates for different types of businesses and verticals.

An easy way to start? Just visit websites from similar companies and see how they organize their content. Most websites will have a section called "About" and a "Contact" page.

"About" is your company's identity: the history, your mission, what you do and maybe the people.

The contact page should include your phone number, email, address and a map in case you have a physical store.

The website should make it easy for a user to find all the important info. A beauty salon's website should include its opening hours and pricelist in a prominent place as well as an easy way to make an online booking.

Your menu which includes About, Contact and other sections should appear on every page. What is more, the website's design should be consistent; the same components should appear on the same part of the page every time and the user's experience should be predictable. The fact that most websites use more or less the same conventions makes it easy for web users across the world to use any website without having to spend a lot of time and effort on them.

Make your website work
for your goals

As mentioned above, it's always important to think like a customer when designing a website. But you also want to the users of your website to use it in a way that helps you achieve your business goals.

When you start designing your site think about your goals, but also keep in mind what users are looking for and how you can provide value for them. The combination of these two elements – customers' needs and your business goals – is the key to a successful website.

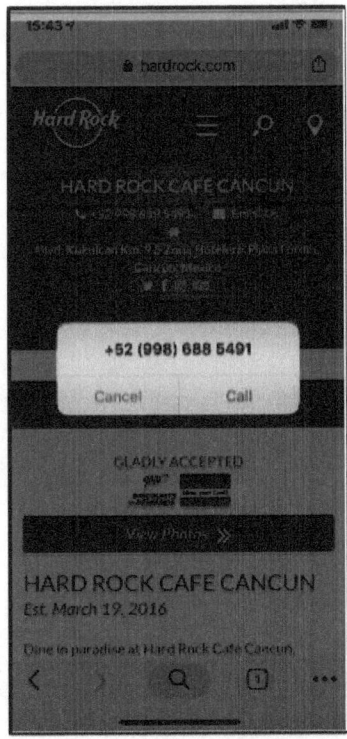

Hard Rock Cafe makes it easy to call any of their restaurants by just tapping on the phone number when you're on mobile.

For example, think about the last time you wanted to find a company's phone number by going to their website. Was it easy to find or did you spend ages looking around?

You should have your phone number on a prominent and visible place on the website. This ensures that your customers don't waste their time when they look for it and that you don't lose customers who can't find your contact info. This sounds intuitive but I've seen many examples of websites getting simple things like these wrong.

Moreover, when someone visits your website from a mobile device make it easy to call your number with just one tap.

Let's go back to our beauty salon example. Your goal is to get people in the local area to visit your business. Your customers want to know how to find you when they want to do a manicure. Again, the simple solution of having a map with directions on your website is a win-win for both.

What else is someone looking on a website? Think about why you usually visit a company's website. Do you want to find out about their prices? Offers? Testimonials?

Make sure you have all of that info available, and you'll be able to serve both your customer's needs and your business goals.

What about content? How should you phrase and write what you want to say on your website? Don't be too technical; people need to understand clearly what you do and how you can help them.

Moreover, don't be too arrogant by claiming you're the best thing that ever happened to them. The customer needs to know how you can solve a problem they have.

Make sure you appeal to a wide audience, so avoid the technical parlance and write in a tone that is confident but without sounding conceited.

As with most pitches (yes, your website is a way to pitch your services), a story helps to make someone understand what you do and root for you. A personal testimonial, a video with a customer's story on how you solved their problem, and reviews will help visitors understand how you can help them.

Finally, remember you're competing for a very short attention span that web users have. Do not overload and clutter your website but make the important things stand out and make sure it is easy to navigate on the site.

Website usability

You've probably been frustrated a few times when you visited a website that was convoluted and hard to use. And I bet that you didn't go back to that website or become a loyal customer of that business.

When it's your turn to create a website, you don't want your users to have this type of experience. You want to make sure the website is easy to use, navigation is simple and clear and that your website makes your customers' lives easier – not more complicated.

Starting with navigation, you want your website to be arranged in a way that is intuitive for your visitors.

When you visit a physical shop, like a grocery store, products are grouped and arranged in a way that makes it easy for people to find the stuff they want. You can organize your products and services in a similar manner on your site; the main menu might include different product categories.

You'll also want to probably include a search bar which is the equivalent of asking an employee at a physical store on where to find a specific product.

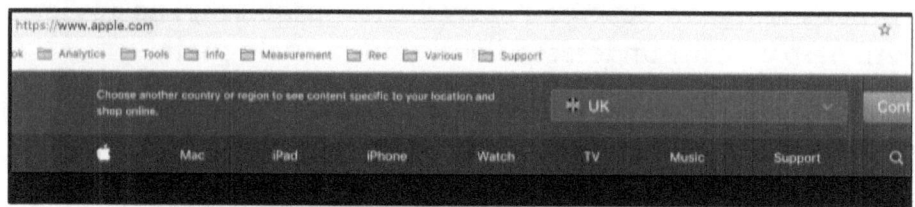

The Apple website menu lists all the different product categories they sell and a search icon.

Make sure the search box is in the same place on every page of your site, so users know where to find it. Consistency is key for a good navigation experience.

Moreover, try to adhere to the design conventions that you can see around the web. For example, when someone clicks on the website's logo (usually on top-left of every page) they expect to be directed to the homepage.

Design is also about style. Everyone has their own taste but there are some rules of thumb that we should also take into account here.

Consistency, once again, is of primary importance. Make sure you use the same color scheme, fonts, images etc. across all pages of your website. This should also align with your brand design, promotional and marketing activities and the image you're trying to convey. It's easier for people to remember your brand if you use the same elements over and over (think: Coca-Cola and the color red, for instance).

You might think that flashy colors might be attention grabbing, but dark text on white background works best as it's easier on the eye.

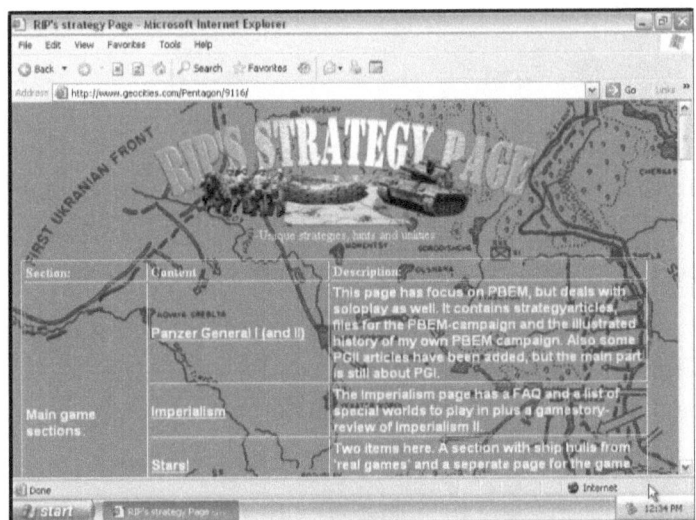

The infamous Geocities websites rarely followed good design rules. Compare them to today's minimalist, mostly white and uncluttered websites.

Remember that people want to consume content mainly on the space that is visible on their screen when they first load the page. Scrolling too far down on the page will deter users from reading all your content. Headers and lists will help them decide if there's something on your site worth their time.

Always write content in the parlance that your audience understands. Are you selling medical equipment and targeting only doctors or clinics? Feel free to include medical and technical jargon. However, if your customer is everyone, keep it simple.

You've probably heard the term "call to action". This means that the website encourages the user to take a specific action, be it signing up for a newsletter, buying a product or booking an appointment.

Make sure the wording you use for those actions is succinct and specific and it features in a prominent place. Do you want people to call you on the phone? Write "Call now" in big letters. Want them to visit your store? Use a "Get directions to our store" banner.

First impressions matter

There are literally billions of websites in the world nowadays, which means that you have to compete for a limited attention span of the average web user. You should at least avoid some common mistakes that drive people away.

Firstly, make sure your website loads fast. Long gone are the dial-up Internet days when you would wait for several minutes for a page to load. Now, even a few seconds can be the deciding factor for a user leaving your website.

According to some studies and anecdotal evidence users won't wait for more than 2-3 seconds for a page to load.

Apart from technical and hosting details which can speed up your website, there are some non-technical fixes for your site's speed.

First, compress your images. Use the smallest possible resolution you need. If you're going to use an image as a thumbnail, you don't need a high-res version of it. Image editing software can help you with this and they usually have a web-friendly option when you save an image.

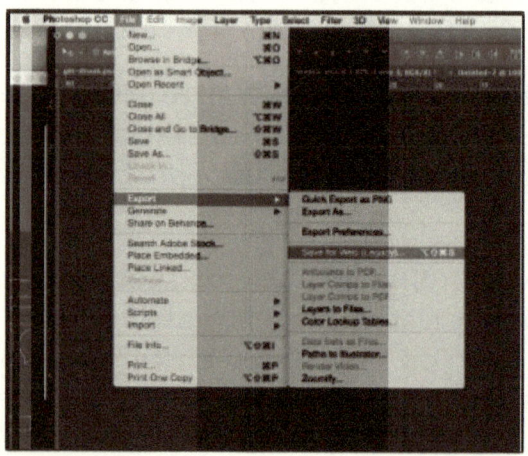

Popular image editing software Photoshop has a "Save for Web" option.

Remember that browsers request all the files from a server when a user wants to visit your website. The simpler the design of your site, the less data the server needs to send to the browser, making the load time faster.

Use the same background image for all your pages on the website, so that only one picture is sent from the server.

Also, test your website. Open it on a mobile device on a 3G and 4G data plan as it might be slower than WiFi. You should accommodate all different users and not just the best-case scenarios.

Similarly, remember that people nowadays use their mobile phone as their primary Internet browsing device. Designing a website for different devices is known as "responsive design", i.e. a website that will work on desktop, mobile, tablet and all kinds of devices, browsers and screen resolutions. This design will adapt to the screen being used and will be displayed accordingly. For example, your website should appear vertically on a mobile device, whereas it will have the standard landscape display on a desktop browser.

Playstation.com will display differently on a desktop and mobile browser. Notice the differences like less text on mobile but also the fact that the important elements like the "Discover PS4" call-to-action button are visible in both cases.

Once again, test your website on different devices. Tools like Google's Mobile-Friendly Test tool (https://search.google.com/test/mobile-friendly) make it easy to check if your website is mobile friendly.

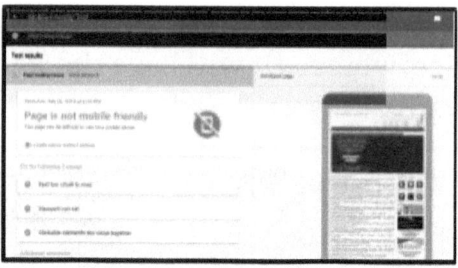

According to the Google Mobile-Friendly Test tool, the website of Greece's Ministry of Foreign Affairs is not optimized for mobile devices. The tool points out specific issues that need to be fixed.

Also, remember that controls like tapping or swiping are unique to touchscreens. Your website should respond to this kind of input by the user. What is more, use icons that are consistently used across the web for certain actions (e.g. a magnifying glass for the "search" function).

If you want people to visit your physical store, make sure that your address and phone number are clearly visible and it's easy to tap on the phone number and call directly on a mobile device.

As with different devices, test your website for different browsers. Chrome, Firefox, Safari and other browsers will not always render the same website in the exact same manner. The same goes for different operating systems, Windows, Mac or Linux.

And always test the website from a user's perspective. Try to take the steps that a user would take and ask why they're here in the first place.

What problem are they trying to solve? Are they looking for a plumber? If yes, is it easy for them to find what they're looking for on a plumber's website?

Ask your friends to test the website. Getting a different perspective will help you fix issues that you hadn't thought about.

YOUR ONLINE STRATEGY

Why have an online strategy?

Starting without an online strategy means that you are less likely to achieve your goals as you are not taking the right steps.

In order to make sure your goals are on track, you need to focus on the key points that are most relevant to them.

The first and most important step is to actually define what you'd like to achieve. Your online goals should align with your business goals. Furthermore, your goals should be specific, e.g. I want to increase my revenue by 15% next year.

A company mission will also help you understand what your business offers and can act as your north star. Simple statements usually work better and guide you to your goals.

Related to your mission is your Unique Selling Point; what is it exactly that makes you stand out from the competition? Why would anyone choose you and not other similar companies?

It might be your price, your exquisite customer service or some products that are not offered by others in your area. This should be your centerpiece of your marketing when you want to convince people to choose you over others.

Some typical goals for an online strategy include increasing sales (e.g. by utilizing your online shop and advertising on various channels), increasing awareness (social media is a great way to do this), get more people to sign up for your newsletter etc.

Start by identifying your business goals and make sure your online strategy is aligned to them.

Differences between the on-line and offline world

How does a customer online act differently from how they be-have in a physical shop? Let's say you want to get fit. In the phys-ical world, you might identify new sneakers as an item that will help you be a better runner and get fit.

You'd go to several sneaker stores, talk to the staff and base your decision on factors like price, staff friendliness etc. After you compare the different options and products, you'll return to the store you'd like the best and buy your sneakers of choice.

In the online world, there is a framework popularized by Google known as "See, Think, Do, Care". This framework has four dis-tinct stages.

First, in the See stage, you might see on social media that your friends post pictures of participation in marathons and that influences you to start running. Next, in the Think stage, you search online advice about running and also read about running shoes. Based on your searches, you see ads and content relevant to running and running shoes.

After hours of research and reading, you decide to buy a pair of shoes from an online shop (Do stage). But your journey doesn't end there. There is also the Care stage, where now you are the one posting pictures of yourself running and winning medals.

Not every online user goes through all four stages. Someone who is already a seasoned runner might go directly to the Do stage and just buy the shoes they like. Or someone else might start from the Think stage and finally end up on Do.

But the reality is that in most cases people act both in the physical and online world. Let's say you are in the sneaker store checking some shoes. You're interested in the new Adidas shoes, so you search for them on your phone to see if you can find a better price elsewhere. It is actually likely that you might end up buying the shoes online although you first saw them in a physical store.

How do you know then what activities to carry out online? To identify the right platforms and channels, you need to figure out your audience, what they're interested in and what their online behavior is.

You can identify different types of audiences (known as audience segments) based on various criteria, e.g. age, gender, interests etc. For example, think about a company selling soccer shoes. There is an obvious audience of young people playing soccer who are interested in the latest fancy shoes advertised by their favorite soccer players, and there is another audience which consists of parents who want to buy something affordable and safe for their kids who play soccer.

Those two audiences are both interested in a sports company's products but in very different ways. You should use different messages and targeting for the two audiences. Online platforms like Google and Facebook can help you show different ads to different people based on demographic characteristics or interests etc.

We'll see how to do this in detail later in this book.

Customer behavior

The center of your strategy should be your customers. They are the ones who will determine the success or failure of your business, and it's important to understand what behavior they display.

Any interaction between your customer and your business is called a touchpoint in marketing parlance. Anything from an ad (viewing or clicking on it), a purchase or a customer support chat they had with your business is a touchpoint and has an impact on how the customer will see your business.

In order to understand your users, you need to find out which touchpoints take place on their customer journey and where exactly they happen.

Once again, try thinking as a customer. What steps exactly and in what order does it take to go through a full journey, from becoming aware of the business to buying something and becoming a loyal customer.

Once you know all the steps, e.g. search for a specific service on Google, go on the company's website, ask for a quote, get a call back etc. you can optimize every step in the journey to make sure you get the most out of every touchpoint and maximize your performance and chances for success.

Moreover, ask yourself the question a user would have when they are faced with a problem that your business can solve. For example, if you own a beauty salon, consider what a potential customer would think about.

This could include questions like: how do I find a beauty salon in my area, how do I learn about new beauty services and techniques, what kind of beauty products are available and which ones are the best for me, how do I choose a brand over another etc.

Moreover, you can ask customers on how they found your business and what journey they took. A survey can give you valuable data but also asking customers face-to-face can be helpful.

Think about adapting your online presence so that it meets your customers' needs and experience. Does my website fulfill the goal that users have when they visit it? Are the online channels that I own actually used by my customers? Am I buying ads on platforms that my potential customers actually use?

Your online strategy should be dynamic and be reviewed once in a while, especially by checking your analytics and see how your touchpoints are performing and if they're still relevant. For example, if your audience starts using a new social platform you should consider creating a profile and interacting with your users on that new social network.

Your digital unique selling points

How do people choose a brand or a shop? Let's say you're looking to buy sneakers. What makes you choose Nike over other brands or a specific sports shop on a street filled with countless other shops?

Maybe you're influenced by the famous athletes wearing Nike shoes or their sneakers fit better to your foot. And you choose a specific retailer because it's convenient or maybe because the staff is polite and helpful.

These – often small – differences can make a shop stand out. The same goes for digital. Your USP (Unique Selling Point) is what will drive people to your business online.

A USP is any clear benefit you offer, what makes you different and why you might appeal to a specific niche.

In order to identify your USP you need to ask who your target audience is (it rarely is everyone and that's a common mistake that brands make), who your competition is, what are the problems that your target audience has, and how can you solve those problems.

As soon as you answer the questions above you can formulate a statement that represents what you company is good at and why someone should choose you. Don't be formal but instead try to think how you would talk about a brand you love to a friend of yours and why you use their products.

Your USP should be your guide for your marketing content on the various platforms that you'll choose to use. Make sure your USP is prominent on your website, social media etc. Remember that you can rarely appeal to everyone; USPs are made to differentiate you from the competition.

You might also have heard about the SWOT Analysis framework which can be helpful when assessing your USPs. SWOT stands for Strengths, Weaknesses, Opportunities, Threats. You must answer the following questions that correspond to these 4 points:

- What are we good at? (strengths)
- What are we not doing well enough and needs improvement? (weaknesses)
- What is something that we can take advantage of to improve and grow? (opportunities)
- What internal or external factors could hinder our growth? (threats)

Chances are that you're not the first business to do what you're currently doing. Competition is not just a force that fights for the same pie as you, but it's also a place to find inspiration and acquire valuable knowledge to improve your own business.

When it comes to the online world, you should check what your competitors are doing. Use search engines to see who the most popular companies are when you search for a certain keyword relevant to your business.

Look at their website and read their content. What kind of keywords do they use and what makes their content stand out?

Follow them on social media and check what kind of content they post and how they communicate with customers.

Moreover, always keep up to date with your industry. An easy and hassle-free way to do this is create Google Alerts for specific keywords.

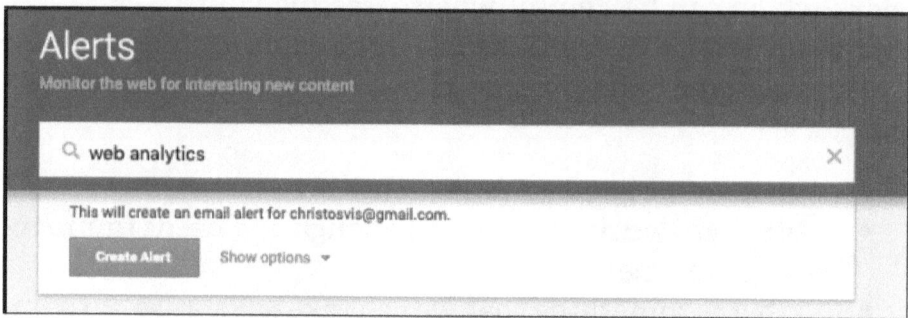

Creating an alert for "web analytics" means I'll get all the relevant news for this field in my inbox.

You can also track your own business and brand on Google Alerts to see if your company is getting traction or what kind of PR is being shared for your company on the web.

Setting and tracking your goals

Goal-setting is a crucial aspect of performance tracking. Without it you don't know where you're going as a business and how you can improve.

Let's start with another business jargon term. KPIs, or Key Performance Indicators are the metrics that you use to evaluate your progress.

Choosing the right KPIs is really important because measuring the right metric means that you are taking actions towards meeting your goals, whereas if you choose a meaningless (for your business) KPI you will be wasting your time into trying to fulfill a goal that doesn't make sense for your business.

Throughout my career as a web analyst and digital marketer I've seen many businesses – big and small – choosing the wrong KPIs which leads to poor business performance.

Often, we refer to this kind of KPIs as "vanity metrics" as they don't really matter for your business. For example, an ecommerce business should have sales as its primary goal. Choosing Facebook page likes as its KPI might make the people who work on the social media page feel good about getting more followers and post likes but in the end what matters is how many sales the marketing team achieved through the various activities.

If getting Facebook likes doesn't lead to more sales, then it's just a metric that distracts you from your main business goal and uses resources that could be better allocated elsewhere.

A good KPI should be measurable and align with your business goals. Let's say you have a gym. Your business goal is to increase your customer base to 100 paid members per month.

To achieve this goal, you need to set your KPIs. This could be reaching out to 30 potential customers (also known as leads) per day, upsell 10 regular memberships per month to premium memberships, and make sure that you reply to all queries by email and social media within 30 minutes.

Setting these very specific KPIs will help you track your results and evaluate your business performance (and your employees). KPIs should reflect actions that help you achieve your goals.

Moreover, when you set them remember the acronym SMART – Specific, Measurable, Achievable, Realistic, Time-Related.

For example, saying that you want to be the top bike shop in your city is neither specific nor measurable and there is no defined time frame for this goal. Instead of a vague phrasing like this, think of what "top bike shop" means for you. It could be "in the next year we want to increase our sales by 50% compared to last year" or "sell 200 bikes per month for the next 6 months".

KPI-setting and evaluation should be a constant process. If the KPI you initially thought would be realistic seems totally out of reach after a few weeks you should review it and adjust it to reflect your day-to-day operations.

Ideally, your KPIs should challenge you and your employees but without being extreme. A healthy year-to-year growth is a good benchmark for your business to track against.

SEARCH ENGINES

Search engine fundamentals

You've all used or at least heard of Google and other search engines like Bing and Yahoo. The core function of search engine is as follows: a user wants to find something, so they type in some keywords or a phrase (or search query in Internet jargon), e.g. "kebab shop in Soho, London" or "what is the capital of Ecuador" or "how to make a DIY arcade cabinet".

The search engine has a vast index of webpages that tries to match with the user's query. Then, then search engine will display the top results on a search page.

The goal of the search engine is to figure out what the most relevant results to your query are so you can find what you're looking for. Whereas most websites aim to keep you on their page for a long time, a search engine's goal is to direct you to some other website in the least time possible. If you spend too much time going through the search result pages, it means that the search engine is not doing a good job!

Search results can be websites, maps, images, ads, items for sale, videos etc.

But what does this mean for your business? Let's assume you own a beauty parlor (as we've done in most cases throughout this book). If a person searched for Jennie's Beauty Parlor (assuming you own this shop) you want your business to appear on the top results of the search page.

And even when someone is searching for something more generic but related to your shop (e.g. manicure, massage in your area) you still want your website to show up on the search results.

The keywords above show the user's intent to buy a service that you're selling. The users searching for those services are the ones most likely to convert to a customer for your business. Naturally, you and the other business that sell the same services have a really strong incentive to appear in relevant search results.

This also means that competition for the first page of Google search results can be fierce. As the old joke goes "the best place to hide a body is page 2 of Google search results". People will usually pick one of the results that show up on the first page of their query (that's roughly 10 results most of the time), so making sure you have a place in those top results can be a critical factor of success.

The mechanics of online search

All search engines' internal mechanics are pretty similar. First, the crawl the web (inspect pages on the Internet to see their content), then they index the content (catalog all the pages and content they see), and finally, they rank the pages (figure out what the most relevant pages is for a given search).

Every search engine has programs called bots, crawlers or spiders that go through millions of websites to discover content. The bots follow the links from page to page, like an explorer would follow new trails to see where they lead to. All the content found by the bots is then indexed and the search engine uses this enormous index to pick the results for the search page that you see when you make a query.

If the search engine finds duplicates of the same page, then it will not add all of them to the index. For example, if you copy the content of another website chances are that your website might not make it to the index and thus, to the search results.

The final part of the mechanism is ranking. When you submit a query, Google might show literally millions of results.

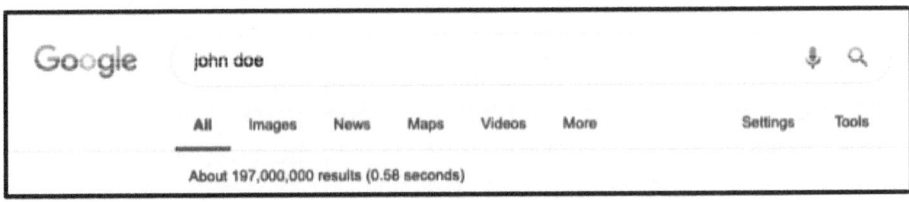

When I search for "john doe" Google comes up with 197 million re-sults in less than a second. That's pretty fast...

But how does it determine which ones to show first and in what order? Google uses an algorithm called PageRank to rank web pages (in reality, PageRank is not the only algorithm used by Google, but it is the most prominent). Although PageRank and other search engine algorithms are secret, the ultimate goal of search engines is to provide the user with the most useful and relevant results.

We'll see in the next chapters how to make the most out of search for your business and how to optimize your web presence to show up in your potential customers' searches.

Optimize your website for search engines

In order for your website to make it to a search engine's index, the search engine needs to know what your page is about. Search engines categorize pages based on their content so that they show up for relevant searches.

But how does a search engine know what your page is about? When a search engine goes through your website it does not only see the content you, as a user, see on screen, but it also sees the code (called HTML) behind the page.

There are some parts of this code that give more info to the search engine. So, which are those parts?

First, you have the title of the page. It's important it represents your website, so in most cases it would be the name of your business, e.g. Jennie's Beauty Salon.

Instead of editing the HTML code yourself you can use programs called CMS (Content Management Systems) that will handle the coding for you. Many of those programs, like Joomla and Word-Press, are free and open-source, so there's a ton of templates and resources you can use for your website.

Next is the text on your page. You should align the content to the keywords and phrases people use to search for your services on Google and other search engines. For example, let's say you have a sneaker store and decide to open a branch in Britain. Most people will search for the term "trainers" instead of "sneakers" for sports shoes in Britain, so you should include those keywords in the content of your website.

Moreover, your website will most probably include images. Search engines don't actually see or understand the images on your website like we do but you can help them figure out what the image is about by adding code behind them.

First, name your images so that the title represents what the image is about. Image.png is not a very good name as you might have guesses, but short-sleeved-yellow-shirt.jpg is a much better name which will help the search engine show your product to someone who's searching for yellow shirts with short sleeves.

Apart from the title of the image you can also add what is known as an "alt tag" to your image. The alt tag will be used in cases that the image cannot be displayed in the browser or for people with visual impairment who can listen to the content instead of reading it.

If you want to edit the HTML yourself, you can add an alt tag like below:

```
<img src="short-sleeved-yellow-shirt.jpg" alt="Short sleeved yellow shirt">
```

However, as mentioned above a content management system will help you add alt tags to images without having to write any code.

Another type of tags included in websites that is used for search is called meta tags. In search engine results a title is used to generate the first line shown on the results and the meta description is used for the few sentences below.

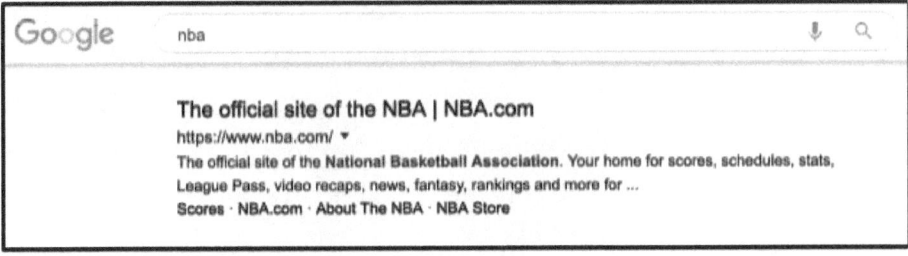

Title and meta description when I search for the term "nba". The first line ("The official site of the NBA…") is the title whereas the two lines below the link are the meta description ("The official site of the […] fantasy, rankings and more for)

Your website should include a clear descriptive title but also a couple of sentences in the meta description tag that reinforce what you see in the title. The description should always match what the website is about.

What's more, your HTML content includes headings and the regular copy that people see on your page. Headings are visible to people, but they are labeled as headings (again don't worry too much about the technical details; a CMS will do the dirty work for you) and should describe what the webpage is about.

And of course, the copy of the page should include the phrases that people are searching for on Google, but don't overdo it by repeating the keyword and phrases in every sentence. Your content must be readable, useful and enjoyable above all!

Organic search / SEO

Organic or unpaid search results appear below the paid results (search ads) on search engines. However, they're still very important for the discovery of your brand by customers.

Let's say your beauty salon is offering a new skin laser treatment. You know that people are looking to buy this service, so they're probably making related queries on search engines.

Although paid search ads will appear above unpaid results, organic results are free, compared to search ads which can cost from a few cents to dozens of dollars depending on the keyword.

Thus, organic results can have a really high return on investment. Their cost is not zero, as you still have to invest time and effort into optimizing them, but you're saving a lot of money that you would otherwise spend on ads.

So, how do you optimize your organic results? As we mentioned above search engines try to find the best match for whatever you're searching. If you can make it clear to the search engine that your page is relevant to the keywords people are using, you have better chances of appearing high in the search results.

The practice of improving your website to gain prominence in organic search results is known as SEO (Search Engine Optimization).

What do SEO best practices dictate? Quality, relevant content. Get into your customers' shoes and try to think what they're searching for. If they're looking for skin treatment they might use it as a keyword, but chances are there are lots of people who are using for a more specific treatment with more criteria (e.g. location, price etc).

Also, they might want to know how the treatment is done, if it's safe etc. You should adjust your content to include the information they're looking for. Moreover, don't copy content from other pages but write your own original content, making sure it includes the keywords people are searching for.

Paid search / SEM

As mentioned in the section above, a search page will display organic (unpaid) results alongside paid search results. The practice of advertising on search engines is called Search Engine Marketing or SEM.

In contrast to traditional media (TV, print, radio) an ad on a search engine is always related to the search a user made. Instead of broadcasting your ad to everyone who happens to be on the medium, the search engine will display different ads for each individual user's queries.

This makes it a lot more likely for a user to click on the ad and convert (purchase something thanks to the ad). Moreover, when you search for something you usually have an intent to buy it or at least, you're already informed about and interested in it.

For example, if you're searching for "Gibson Les Paul guitar" on Google, it means you're already familiar with electric guitars, the brand Gibson and there's some reason why you're searching for it. You want to learn more about it, compare prices on different stores, or see where you can buy it from.

In any case, just by searching for this term you've shared some valuable information about your interests and probably your consumer behavior.

Paid ads have a very similar look and feel to organic results on a search results page and are featured on top which makes them more prominent and more likely to be clicked on.

But how is a search ad served to a user? Every time someone submits a query on a search page there is an opportunity to display ads. Search engines run algorithms on the spot to decide in a fraction of a second which ads and in what order will be displayed on the page.

The main factors for deciding on which ads to display are the bid and the quality of the ad. The bid is the maximum amount and advertiser is willing to pay for a click on an ad (ads that are charged on a per click basis are also known as Cost-per-click / CPC or Pay-per-click / PPC ads).

When you click on an ad the advertiser might actually pay less than what their bid, but they will never pay more than it. Moreover, they will only pay when someone clicks on their ad.

So, let's say you're running a search ad with a bid of $1 per click. If no one clicks on your ad you won't be charged at all. If only one person clicks on your ad, you'll be charged $1 or less for that click.

How do you know what a keyword is worth to you? There are two things to consider here. First, the competition. Some keywords are really expensive, because many companies are willing to bid top dollar for them.

But in order to know if it's worth paying a high bid for a keyword you should determine a click's worth to your business. And how do you do that? By testing and analyzing data.

Start with running some ads for a keyword relevant to your business. In the case of a beauty salon, let's say you decide to bid for "manicure near me". You get 100 clicks and 10 conversions (purchases) thanks to your ad. Let's assume that every manicure generates a $20 revenue, but $12 of it is cost, so the profit is $8. You decide that out of this $8 profit you're willing to spend $5 on marketing, so that in the end you have a $3 profit (but hopefully you'll drive a lot more customers to your business).

In this case, you're willing to pay $5 on a conversion for a manicure. Since you need 10 clicks to generate a conversion, you shouldn't bid more than 50 cents for a click ($5 cost per conversion / 10 clicks).

As you gather more data you should revisit this approach and adjust your cost per conversion and cost per click so that it is reflected in your search ads bid.

Obviously, the numbers above are illustrative only, but you get the idea. Sometimes, you might be willing to minimize your profit (thus increasing your bid even more than $5 in our example) in order to grow your customer base.

In order for the search engines to decide which ad is shown to a user based on their query an auction takes place. But it's not just the monetary bid that determines the outcome of the auction.

Quality is also very important. Search engines will assign a score to every ad based on their relevance to the user's search. As a matter of fact, an ad with really relevant content can beat other ads that might have a higher bid.

What's more, some ads might not appear at all even if they have a really high big, If they're not relevant to the search.

Thus, quality is important because it can help you win auctions and appear on the search results. Another implication is that if your content is really relevant to the search you can save money by bidding less as the quality / relevance of your ad will compensate for the lower bid.

So, remember to invest in quality content for your page. It will help you appear higher both in paid and organic search results.

SEM might require a budget – compared to free organic search traffic – but used wisely it can bring amazing results with a high return on investment for your company, and it will target customers at the very time they search for a service that you provide.

How to use Google Search Console

Throughout the book we're going to present some tools that you can use to optimize your online performance. As we've mentioned, most of them are free to use!

Google Search Console (https://search.google.com/search-console/welcome) is a tool by Google that you can use to track your performance in Google Search results and find out how you can improve your visibility.

First, you have to add your website to the search console and verify it following the instructions.

A few days after you verify your site you'll start seeing data in the reports.

The first one is called "Performance report" and shows how your site performs in Google results, how many clicks and impressions you get for various keywords, the average position in search results etc.

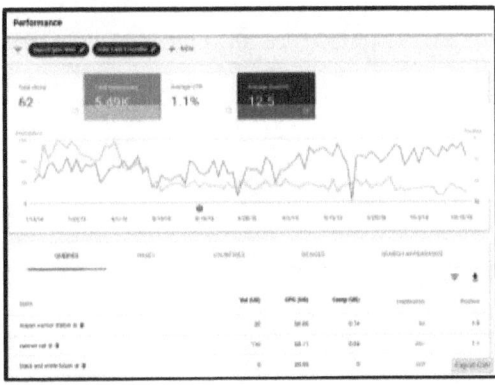

The performance report in Google Search Console

Use this report to evaluate different queries and how they perform. For example, let's say you are a fitness trainer and want to find out how people search for your services. You might see a big difference in performance for variations of the same theme, e.g. "fitness training", "training for a beautiful body", "classes to get fit". If one of them outperforms the rest you should consider focusing on that keyword more than the others when, for example, bidding for search ads.

Moreover, this will help you adjust your content on your webpages so that it includes more of the best-performing keywords.

You can also see how people's behavior is different on different devices, and check if people search for images, websites or videos.

Another thing to look for is if your site comes up on search results but gets no clicks. That means that your content is not actually what people are looking for when searching for a specific keyword.

The Links report shows websites that link to your site. Those are also known as referrals and it's always good to know which site is directing people to your site.

Make sure you check the "Mobile Usability" report as well. Mobile has become the de facto way to use the web due to the omnipresence of smartphones, so this report will help you find out if any of your pages don't work well on mobile phones.

Build your SEO plan

Now that you understand how search engines work, you should create an SEO plan that aligns with your goals.

Let's say you run a hip organic foods store. What kind of keywords do people use when searching for this kind of product?

Organic food? Gluten-free? Fresh? Do they want to know if such stores deliver their products in the area?

Moreover, what kind of topics would a potential customer be interested in? Do they want to know about vegan diets? Gluten-free recipes? Health benefits of a vegetarian diet?

Now that you've narrowed down your list of keywords to more specific ones that match your customers' needs and searches. This brainstorming and ideation should be done on a regular basis (e.g. every 6 months) to update your SEO plan based on how your business is evolving, but also the different trends that people are following.

After compiling your list of keywords, see how you're performing for them in search results. Does your website show up on Google search for all of those keywords? Are there particular topics that don't bring people to your website?

This will help you find out what is performing well. If certain popular keywords don't bring traffic to your website, you can include them to your SEO plan.

Next, you should fix the gaps that you just identified. A common problem is a lack of links from other sites pointing to your site. Maybe, you can build a community of foodie and vegan bloggers who can write about your shop. You can invite them to try some of your products and write a review.

SEO takes time so you should thing about the short and long-term. In the short term, make sure you write some articles on the topics missing from your site.

For the long term, you might add bigger actions to your SEO plan, like redesigning your website and adding entire sections of related topics to it.

Your plan will change and adjust over time, especially when you make changes to your business, e.g. when introducing a new product or when you have a new website.

Moreover, try to keep up with the search engine trends. Google regularly makes changes to their algorithm and announces them so that people know what the best SEO practices are. For example, mobile has grown increasingly more important over the last years, so it should be a top consideration for the design of your website.

Finally, track your performance (e.g. by using Google Search Console) and make changes when something's not working. Do you see that certain pages don't get traffic anymore? You could refresh the content and update your keywords.

Do you find that people come to your website, but they don't buy products? It might be that your calls to action are not strong enough. Test your content and keywords and see which ones perform better.

Constantly monitoring your performance and adjusting your actions accordingly is the core of a good digital marketing strategy – not just SEO.

Remember that the Internet offers a ton of resources on topics like SEO. Find blogs that you like and follow them. They'll help you keep up-to-date with algorithm changes and SEO trends.

Feel free to copy the strategy of other successful websites. If something works for them, you should consider it as well, be it social media activity, new content trends etc.

And don't forget to get customer feedback. They know what they want better than any marketing plan.

How to pick the right keywords

SEO is about keywords. The right ones will set your SEO plan for success.

Your content should match what people search for on Google and other search engines. If that's not the case your website is not living up to your users' expectations. They search for one thing and when they click on the search result the content is about something else.

This creates a negative experience. This type of traffic might even backfire for you: users might complain that about your company or associate it with a bad experience.

In order to select the right keywords, think about the following criteria:

1. Frequency (how many times a word is searched for): You want to include the words and phrases that people search for the most often (always, in relation to your business; don't try to include irrelevant keywords just because they're popular. This creates the kind of negative experience described above).

2. Competition: Obviously popular keywords will lead to many businesses competing for them. However, if you're not a big and established business with lots of traffic to your website you might want to focus on the "long tail" keywords, i.e. keywords with a smaller volume of searches. Usually those are more niche or specific keywords and are called long-tail because keywords usually consist of a few high-volume terms and a very large list of low-frequency terms. Both are important for SEO. The long tail is where a small busi-

ness will find an SEO opportunity.

3. Relevance: The keywords you choose should represent the content you have on your website. Don't try to deceive your users by selecting a keyword that brings traffic but then the content is irrelevant. Moreover, the way search algorithms work, even if you manage getting some traffic for the "wrong" keyword, it won't last for long, since seach engines rank the results based on relevance. So, in SEO, misbehavior doesn't pay off!

Remember to use Google Search Console to evaluate your keywords. What's more the content should be made for humans and not search engines. Sometimes, especially in the past, people tried or try to game the system by creating pages that will rank high based on the keywords they include although their content is almost useless for any real person.

Even if this worked at some point it's a tactic that doesn't work anymore and won't get you anywhere.

Another, risky and not very successful method of trying to manipulate search results is called "keyword stuffing" where you'd repeat the same keyword over and over hoping you'll get better search results. Please don't do that! Not only does it create ugly content but it's also against search engine guidelines. Those tactics will only ensure your page is not displayed in search results.

An example of keyword stuffing on Google's help center is:

"We sell custom cigar humidors. Our custom cigar humidors are handmade. If you're thinking of buying a custom cigar humidor, please contact our custom cigar humidor specialists at custom.cigar.humidors@example.com."

When you see something like this, always ask yourself: would I, as a user, find this type of content useful and appealing? Good digital marketing boils down to thinking like a real person using your website.

Your SEO goals

In order to understand how your website is performing in organic search results and ensure that it aligns with your business goals, you need SEO goals.

Moreover, you should track your performance in analytics to make improvements and learn.

Start by asking what it is you want to achieve online and how you define success. Let's say you are an organic foods store owner. Your goals are conversions (getting people who visit to website to buy your products) and acquisition (finding new customers).

Setting goals will help you measure that what you're doing is relevant and useful for your business. Assume you're ranking number one in search engine results for "organic vegetables". You see that you get lots and lots of visitors to your website, but they don't necessarily convert.

What does this mean? Maybe people are searching for "organic vegetables" for the "wrong" reason – wrong for your business goals, that is. Maybe people use those keywords to plant vegetables in their back yard and not buy from you.

If a keyword is not doing what you intended, it to do for your business goal then ditch it. Replace it with a narrower and more specific keyword or an altogether different theme.

Moreover, being number one on a search page is probably not your primary goal for SEO. Instead, it is a means to an end. And the end is always your business goal. That's how you will ultimately measure success.

But how are you going to measure the business goal – purchases in your case? You can track the actions of your users on your website, so every time someone comes from a certain keyword and buys something this will show up on your analytics tool. If tracking purchases is difficult (for example you own a beauty salon and people have to come to your store to buy your services) you can track another action that is close to a purchase, for example the completion of a signup form for booking an appointment with your business.

Search engines like Google provide these analytics tools for free (e.g. Google Search Console that we saw above) and you should be monitoring reports like the ones that show you which keywords bring people to your site, how many people click the links etc.

Moreover, by using analytics tools like Google Analytics (we'll talk about this tool later) you can find out how many organic visitors become paying customers, which content is or is not performing well and much more.

Take advantage of other websites

SEO is impacted by things that happen on your website but also on things that happen on other websites. This happens because whatever other websites are saying about your site is taken into account by search engines.

The two major categories where this happens is backlinks and social media.

A backlink is any link from another website to your site. For search engines, a backlink acts as a vote: having a lot of sites linking to your site means that your site is seen as a trusted website with good content.

Search engines take a note of those backlinks and interpret it as a sign of high-quality content and will place you higher in the page results.

As with most things related to SEO, the important factor is quality and not quantity. In the past, people tried to game the system by getting a ton of backlinks which in many cases were irrelevant to the content or came from websites that had minimal content and were built only as a repository of backlinks for other websites.

When search engines discovered this practice, they changed their policy by making sure those websites – also known as "link farms" as their sole purpose was to be full of backlinks – would get less value in the rankings.

Search engines will always respond to shady SEO practices by changing the way the value pages, so keep that in mind and always focus on quality.

For backlinks, the important thing is that you get links that come from trusted sites and are legit.

So, how can you get backlinks that provide value in search results? As in most cases your content is the defining factor. If your content provides value – either educational, informational or entertaining – other people will link to it as they believe their audience should see it. Encouraging others to share your content and link to your website is also part of this strategy.

Good content has the end user in mind and what can help them find information, help or just be entertained by a great piece.

The other way to promote your content and get links is, of course, social media. Search engines will crawl all pages they can see on the web including social media. They won't give you extra points for having lots of followers, fans or likes. But using social media is a great way to get more people to notice your content and business and link to your website. Good content can spread quickly on social media (or go viral as some like to call the effect of getting a piece of content become massively popular in a short time) and generate links for your site.

We'll cover social media later in the book, but for the time being remember that what other people say about your business on the web is important and can help you rank higher on search engines.

As always, good content, is king for SEO.

Going international with SEO

If you have potential customers in many different countries or operate in areas where multiple languages are spoken, then you have to adjust SEO to those elements.

First and most importantly, you need to make sure your SEO is in the same language as the one that your customers use.

If you have a business in California or Florida, you probably deal with Spanish and English-speaking customers (probably also Chinese and other languages but let's keep the example simple for now). Your website should have a separate page (URL) for each language. The reason is that although you can use a widget on your page that translates the content automatically, search engines crawling the website will only see the original version of the page.

So, let's say you have a page with the URL www.examplebeautysalon.com/manicure for your beauty salon in Florida and the page is in English. You should have a separate page for Spanish speakers, something like www.examplebeautysalon.com/es/manicure or www.examplebeautysalon.com/manicure-es (you get the point).

That way search engines will be able to crawl both versions of your page and serve them accordingly to users based on what language they use.

Moreover, don't include two different languages on the same page (e.g. the same content in English and Spanish on the same page). When a search engine crawls your page it will be confused (yes, machines can be confused, too) and won't be able to decide if your webpage is in English or Spanish, thus making it hard for the engine to serve the page in search results.

Again, use different pages and URLs for different languages and avoid using automated services for translating your content. Either spend some time translating your content yourself or just hire someone to do it for you.

The translation will be better in quality, but you will also avoid getting lower ranking in search results, as search engines do not value automatically translated content. In many cases, it can be seen as spam by Google and other search engines.

You can also tell Google about your localized version of your page by using the tag *hreflang* in HTML or by using a sitemap. If you don't want to go into technical details a content management system will help you do this, but if you want to implement this yourself you need to add <link rel="alternate" hreflang="lang_code"... > to the page header to tell the search engine what language your page is in.

A sitemap is a file that provides information about your website and all the pages and files that are on it. A search engine should already be able to discover most of this info on its own, but it's always a good idea to have a sitemap. There are many tools that will generate your sitemap for you, and you can submit it to Google through Google Search Console.

These tags will help search engines decide if they will serve your content on the English or Spanish version of search results (for our example).

Aside from languages there are other considerations when you're operating in a multi-national environment. Things like currencies, metric systems, contact details, time zones might alienate your user if they're not in the standard used in their country.

A good website is useful when it lists relevant information for its users, and you should make it easy for search engines and people understand that you're addressing their needs.

For example, if you have operations in different countries you might want to consider buying domains extensions for all of them. For example, if your company operates in France and Italy, you'd want to buy the .fr and .it extensions (that also helps the search engine that this domain is probably the French or Italian version of your website).

However, you might only have a .com website for global use. What happens in that case? How does Google know which country you're targeting?

Google will use factors like where it's hosted, its IP address and other info to determine the country, but you can also help by using the country targeting tools in Google Search Console.

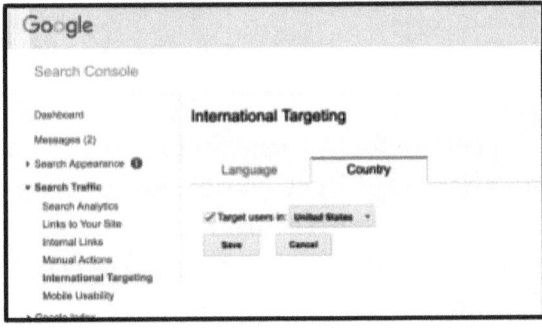

Use Country Targeting in Google Search Console to tell Google which Country you're targeting.

A lot of businesses start by thinking locally but then they realize that going cross-border is the way to grow their business. This applies especially to ecommerce companies as this is a great way to expand. Localization will always be a key factor on whether you succeed entering new markets or not.

Paid search ads revisited

We mentioned that when you do a search you'll be served both paid ads and organic results.

Search results for the term "nike". Note that the first result is an ad whereas the second one is an organic result.

For example, if you perform a search for "nike" the first results will be ads and then you'll get the organic – free- results. Paid ads are always shown first on search results. Paid search results will always be marked as ads but other than that they're very similar in appearance with organic results.

Google and other search engines let you bid for keywords and you only pay when someone clicks on the link. That's why this form of advertising is also known as pay-per-click or PPC.

Obviously, one can argue that this makes search ads superior in many ways for ads that are "lower-funnel". If you're not familiar with this marketing term imagine that potential customers go through a funnel of different marketing activities in order to end up buying your product.

In the top of the funnel you have your branding or awareness activity where you're trying to make people aware of your company. In the middle, there is the consideration where you try to make people know your product and become more familiar with your brand. And in the bottom or lower-funnel you have what is known as direct response (DR) or more action-oriented marketing where you're trying to convince people to make a purchase (or take a specific action).

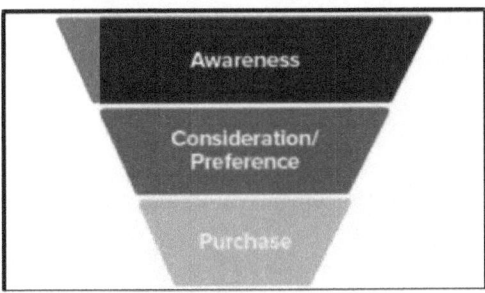

The marketing funnel.

The visualization of this concept resembles a funnel as it is wider on top (you reach a lot of people with brand or awareness campaigns) and narrow at the bottom (only a small percentage of people you reached initially will end up buying your product).

Search ads usually live in the bottom of the funnel as people will come across them when they search for specific keywords. Since this means that people are already interested in the product related to the keyword, they're much more likely to buy it.

This has two benefits for search ads: they will be a lot more relevant to the user than, say, a TV ad where you don't know if the people watching your ad are actually interested to the product.

And, second, the people who search for that keyword already have intent to buy it (in most cases) making search ads a good bang for your buck if used correctly.

Of course, this also has another implication. Since search ads can target "warm" customers there will be a lot of competition with other companies bidding for the same "hot" keywords driving the prices up.

That's why it's important to thoroughly research your keywords and try to find hidden opportunities in the long tail.

Next, we'll explain how the search auction works, which determines which ads will be shown and how much you'll be paying for every click on your ad.

How the search ads auction works

A search results page consists of organic and paid search results. As we mentioned above, paid ads appear on top but there is a limited number of slots for those ads. So, how does Google or other search engines determine which ads are going be included in those slots?

An auction is used to determine which advertisers are going to win the privilege of appearing in the paid search results. And the auction will also determine the order of the ads (winners of the auction will appear on top and runners-up below them), as well as the price that they have pay for every click on their ads.

But how does the auction exactly work? Like in most auctions you place a bid. But unlike other auctions, it's not just the bid that will determine the outcome of the auction. The relevance of your ads is the other factor that will be taken into account as well. Success in the auction is a combination of both those factors.

Let's say you're willing to pay up to $5 for a click on your ad when someone searches for beauty salon related services. This is your maximum cost per click (Max CPC). If your competitors have a Max CPC of $3 then you have a higher bid, thus higher chances of winning the auction. Bids are not set in stone but companies can change them at any time, so you'll need to monitor bids to make sure you're not way behind in the auction.

However, the bid alone will not guarantee you a spot in the search results. What you need to have in conjunction with a competitive bid is relevance. This metric – usually on a scale from 1 to 10 – depicts how closely your ad relates to what a person actually searched for. Google and Bing usually refer to this as Quality Score.

For example, let's assume someone is searching for beauty

salons in Brooklyn and your ad's headline is "Jimmy's Beauty Salon in Brooklyn". This is highly relevant, and you will probably get a high Quality Score.

However, if your ad is about a hair salon this is not as relevant to what the users are searching for, so you'll be assigned a low Quality Score.

Thus, if you have two businesses with the same bid price, the one with the higher quality score will appear higher in the search results page. Relevance can really help you improve your SEM performance without raising your bids.

Let's take another example. Both Alice and Bob bid for the same keyword. Alice bids $5 and has a low quality score, 3 out of 10. Her total auction score (or ad rank) is 5*3=15.

Bob bids less than Alice, only $3, but has a much higher quality score, a perfect 10 out of 10. His score is 3*10 = 30.

Although Bob's bid was less than Alice's, his quality score helped him win the auction and appear higher than Alice on the search results.

This means that you can't just buy your way to the top of search results. This is good both for advertisers and users. Users get to see the ads that have the most value to them and advertisers know they can compete fairly with other businesses. They also have an incentive to make their ads and content relevant to users' searches.

Keep in mind that if your relevance is really low, no matter how high your bid, search engines might not display your results at all.

The conclusion is that you should focus on making your ads more relevant and that they always match what people are searching for. This will save money for your business and improve your performance in SEM.

Good keywords for SEM

The three important factors for good SEM keywords are relevance, traffic and competition. Since you pay every time someone clicks on your ad you want to make sure you're getting a good return on investment for your ads.

Let's revisit our beauty salon example and assume that the keyword "manicure Brooklyn" costs you $3 per click.

If you know the value of this keyword for your business, you can judge if it's worth paying that price on search engines for it.

Of course, in order to know this, you actually have to start a campaign so you can have data on both the cost and value. How do you, however, research keywords before starting to run a campaign for them?

First of all, think if these keywords are relevant to your business and what people are searching for when they want to find the services that you sell.

Do not generalize but focus only the keywords that are closely relevant to your business and what you sell.

Second, think about how much traffic a keyword can generate. Even if a keyword is highly relevant but no one searches for it why would you add it to your keywords?

For example, a very detailed phrase, e.g. "Brooklyn beauty salon with great manicure services in low prices", might describe your business exactly but it's not very likely people will be using this keyword to search for it. As a result, bidding on this keyword won't really bring much traffic to your website.

If you try something like "Brooklyn manicure" you still get a keyword that is relevant to your business but with higher chances of people searching for it.

Keyword research tools like Google Keyword Planner can help you with recommendations but like with most things trial and error will provide you with experience and knowledge.

Google Keyword Planner can give you keyword recommendations.

The last factor you have to take into consideration is competition. If a keyword is relevant and can bring traffic, then other companies that sell the same services as yours are probably using it too.

For example, most beauty parlors in Brooklyn are bidding on the keyword "Brookly beauty salon".

This doesn't mean you should not bid on it, but you should also try to find keywords that are still relevant and can bring in traffic but don't have as much competition.

Maybe something like "Brooklyn gel manicure" might be relevant to a service you offer but might be less competitive (disclaimer: I'm not an expert on manicure, so please be lenient on me when I use it as an example!).

The three aforementioned factors – relevance, traffic, competition – are all important when choosing SEM keywords and you have the right balance that works for your business. At the end of the day, what matters to your business is that you have keywords that bring in more value than they cost when you advertise to them.

Create effective search ads

In order for your ads to perform well they need to stand out of the crowd. If you make a search for a term that you're interested in, you might notice that a lot of the ads look similar. How, then, are you going to make people notice your ad?

Make aa search for a popular term, e.g. "personal trainer". What do you notice? There are probably a lot of personal trainers in your area and the ads seem to say the same thing. Moreover, there are organic results below the ads.

If your ad is not offering something unique, there's a risk it will get lost in the crowd.

There are a few things you can do to stand out. First, relevance. Write the headline of the ad so that it matches the keyword as closely as possible. If you're bidding for the term "hire personal trainer" you can use this as for your headline as it is clear and matches what a potential customer is searching for.

This will also ensure a high relevance score for your ad in the auction.

What else is there that you can use to attract people amidst the competition? Are you running a sale, an offer or a promotion? If yes, this is a great chance to show a competitive advantage (remember when we were talking about unique selling points? Price is one of them) that your business offers.

In the beauty parlor example, something like "Get 40% off your first facial treatment" is a very alluring benefit for people to show interest in your business. Other examples for various industries include "Free Shipping for Purchases over $50", "Get a Free Pump for Every Basketball you Buy" etc.

This already gives an incentive to users to visit your website.

The final thing is what we call a call to action. This is you telling the users what you want them to do when they visit your website. This is really important as people tend to respond to calls to do something specific.

This has to be clear and actionable (hence call to action). It could be "Buy Now!", "Subscribe to our Newsletter", "Take a Test Drive!", "Make a Booking" etc.

Usually your call to action is the second line of your ad, so that the user is directed to take a specific action after they click on the ad. This manages the expectation of the user and directs them to the action you want them to take.

For example, your call to action for your beauty parlor could be "View our Amazing Manicure Gallery". This is an exciting proposition for someone who wants to see examples of manicure ideas and shows the great work that your business is doing.

Laser Eye Surgery | €500 Off Limited Time Offer | optilase.com
[Ad] www.optilase.com/ ▾
Achieve Freedom From Glasses & Get €500 Off Laser Eye Treatment. Book Now! Price Guarantee.

Optilase ad on Google search for the term "laser eye surgery".

Look at this example from Optilase for a laser eye surgery. It has a very relevant title, a special offer that expires ("limited time"), thus urging me to do this as quickly as possible and has a clear call to action ("Book now").

Having a good ad that stands out from the crowd can help your SEM perform better, get more clicks and conversions for your business, and ultimately, get a better return on investment for your search ads. Make Better Ads Now!

Good structure for your
search campaigns

When it comes to relevance search engines take into account not just your ad but also your landing page, i.e. the first page people see after they click on your ad.

This means that your landing pages should also be relevant to what a user is searching for.

How should you structure your SEM campaigns to get great relevance? Your structure has different levels. On the top, there is your account which you create, for example, in Google Ads. Every account can create campaigns. A campaign controls levers like budget, the regions or countries where your ad will appear in, and the advertising networks you want to use.

Every campaign contains ad groups. An ad group is a collection of keywords and ads that run for those keywords.

Structuring your account in this organized manned will help you show the ads with the highest relevance.

For example, if you are the owner of an apparel company and offer different types of clothing (jeans, coats, shirts, dresses), you should probably split them into different campaigns. Every campaign will include ad groups for the different items of every clothing category. For example, your "dresses" campaign might include ad groups for summer dresses, winter dresses etc.

Every ad group will contain related keywords and you can write the ads that correspong to those keywords (e.g. "Summer Dresses | 20% off").

If someone searches for the keywords in this ad group this will be a highly relevant ad.

Organize your campaigns based on the products and services

that you offer and it will make your SEM life a lot easier.

Keyword research

Keyword research tools like Google's Keyword Planner or Bing's Keyword Research Tool can help you in your research for the most relevant keywords for your campaigns.

For example, if you search for the term "meal delivery" in Google Keyword Planner you will see other related searches like "food delivery", "restaurants that deliver near me" etc.

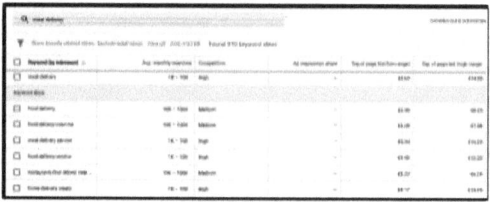

Google Keyword Planner results for "meal delivery".

The tool will also show you how many times a term was searched for, bid prices etc.

On the left side of the tool you can see a section called "Grouped ideas". This will help you create groups of keywords, or ad groups as we saw in the previous section about organizing your campaigns.

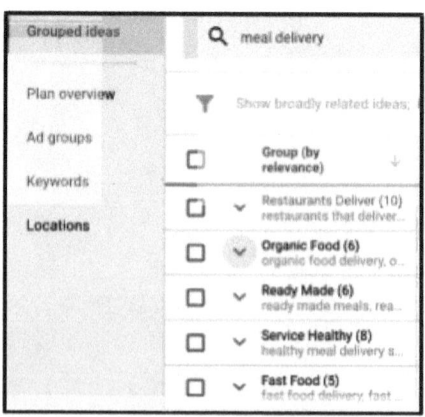

Google Keyword Planner enables you to find groups of similar keywords.

However, there might also be keywords that might not be relevant. In the meal delivery example, there might be keywords that don't have to do with a food delivery business.

In this case, you can use negative keywords, i.e. keywords that will be excluded from your campaigns to make sure that your ads will not be shown when people search something that is not relevant to your business.

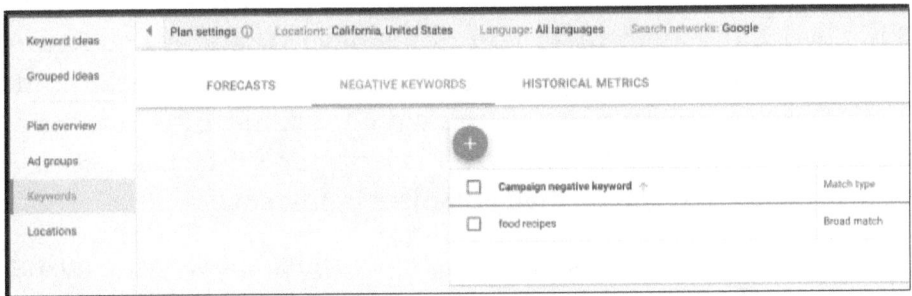

You can include negative keywords to prevent your ads from showing up in searches that might not be relevant.

This tactic is going to save you money as you ensure that your ads will not appear for terms that might seem relevant but don't really contribute to your business results.

Make sure you use keyword tools regularly to see the trends in search terms but also what keywords appear in those searches that might not be relevant.

Search behaviors tend to change over time, so you need to keep an eye on them and accordingly adjust your search campaigns.

Keyword match types

So far, we've seen that search engines will show your ads for specific keywords. But they might also show your ads for other terms that you didn't specifically pick.

This characteristic of search engines – showing your ad for variations of your keyword – is called broad matching.

This is usually helpful as you don't have to add all the variations of a keyword you'd like to target, like the plural number of a keyword or misspellings which is something common. You wouldn't want to miss out on an opportunity just because someone spelled the service you offer incorrectly.

This also means that search engines might show your ad for keywords that might not be relevant to your business. For example, let's say you own an organic foods store. The term "organic foods" might also show your ads to people who are not interested in buying your products. Maybe they're interested in planting and growing their own organic plants.

You could prevent showing your ads to such audience by refining your keywords, e.g. using the term "buy organic foods".

You can also specify if you want to use broad matching, phrase matching or exact matching for your keywords. Keywords are broad match by default. To use phrase match use quotations around the keyword.

Phrase match means that the ad can only be displayed for the entire phrase. So, if someone searches for "buy organic foods" they will be shown the ad. Slight variations, like singulars or plurals, are also acceptable, e.g. "buy organic food" will also show your ad.

But if someone searches just "organic food" your ad won't show up, since you specified that the word "buy" should be included in the phrase. Keep in mind that words before and after the phrase can also trigger the ad, as long as your phrase is included intact in the search. For example, your ad can also be shown for the phrase "buy organic foods in my area".

Exact match is used when you want the search to be exactly what you specified it to be. In order to use exact match, you have to place your keyword in square brackets, i.e. [buy organic food] for our example.

If someone searches for "organic food" your ad will not appear as it doesn't match the keyword exactly.

The difference with phrase match is that if the user includes additional words (e.g. "buy organic foods in my area") the ad won't display, but small variations can (plurals etc) can still qualify for your ad ("buy organic food" instead of "buy organic foods").

It goes without saying that going from broad to phrase to exact matching you're limiting the opportunities for your ad to show up in searches. You should probably not be too restrictive and, as with most things we suggest, you should do your research and testing and strike that balance that allows ads to show to potential customers and limit their appearance when a term becomes unlikely to turn into a purchase.

As you add more phrase and exact keywords you should expect your traffic to go down but the quality of users coming to the website improving (quality in the sense that they're more likely to become paying customers). Once again, you should strive for that balance that will enable you to have good quality prospects without limiting your audience too much. After all, your company needs both good customers and an increasing user base in order for your business to grow.

Tracking your conversions

In order to know if your search ads are working you should track your conversions, i.e. the actions that you want users to take on your website be it product purchases, filling out a form, watching a video etc.

First, how do you define which conversions to track? If you have an e-store, tracking orders is an obvious conversion. But are there any other actions that might be of value to your business?

Your website might have a contact form where people can ask you questions about your products (a good indication that they're interested in buying something from your website), so this could qualify as a conversion. Of course, this type of conversion doesn't have the same value as an order, but it has some value as it shows that a user is "warm".

Another example is signing up for a newsletter, downloading a catalog or clicking to receive your pricelist via email. These actions indicate a meaningful action and can be included in your conversions, as they show that someone has the potential of becoming a paying customer.

Think about what constitutes a meaningful action for your website, something that indicates that a user is closer to purchasing something from your business. These actions, along with actual purchases, should be probably tracked as conversions.

How do you track them then? Search engines allow you to place a small piece of code on pages of your website so that actions that happen on them are tracked by the search engine.

For example, when someone places an order there should be an order confirmation page on your website. A tracking code should be placed on that page – and that page only – to track successful orders. Now, every time someone places an order, the order confirmation page is loaded and, consequently, the corresponding tracking code is triggered. This lets you and the search engine know how many orders occurred.

In general, the tracking code should be placed on a page that is shown only after a certain action has been taken (usually a "thank you" or "confirmation" page).

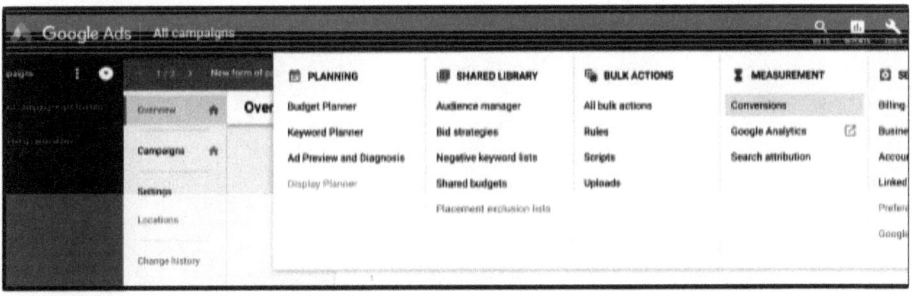

Google Ads lets you define your conversions in Tools > Measurement > Conversions.

For example, Google Ads enables you to define all your conversions and their types (purchases, leads, sign-ups etc) as well as their value. The tool will generate a tag – a piece of code – that you need to paste in the <head> section of the confirmation page that makes sense for the conversion. As we mentioned above, implement the code only on the page where the confirmation of the conversion happens and nowhere else.

This is a pretty straightforward thing to do for someone who knows HTML – it literally takes a minute or so – but if you have trouble implementing it ask someone's help. Remember that Google is full of step-by-step tutorials on how to implement a tag.

This book does not intend to turn you into a web developer, but we instead prefer to focus on the marketing part. However, if you feel like tracking codes is something you enjoy and want to learn how to implement it is relatively simple to learn how to add basic tags on your website.

Once you have these tracking codes on your web pages, you'll start getting data which will help you measure your campaigns' performance.

DIGITAL MARKETING FOR LOCAL BUSINESSES

Location, location, location

If you run a physical store local customers or people visiting your local area are the ones bringing revenue to your business.

When we say local, we mean either businesses with a shop (musical instruments shop, beauty parlor) or professional services that are offered in an area (plumbers, electricians etc).

Usually, their customers are people who live in their vicinity but it's not necessary. Someone might be a tourist and need to visit a dentist (unfortunate but it happens) on while on vacation, or they might be driving from a small town to your big town to visit your bike shop as there is no such business in their area.

In the past, people would use the phone book to find businesses in their area that offer the kind of products or services they're interested in. Nowadays, people will just use their computer or smartphone to perform a local search.

Let's say you're looking for a store that repairs musical instruments. You'll probably search something relevant on Google and specify that it's for your area, town or region. You'll get a list of music stores with relevant info like the address, contact detail and opening hours.

If you're on mobile you can click on their phone number to instantly call the store or use Google Maps or Apple Maps (or any other maps app) to get directions for the store.

So, how can you make sure people find your local business?

First, make sure you have your address and a map along with other contact details on your website. Working hours and a telephone should also be included.

If you serve only specific areas make sure to mention it very clearly in your contact details.

In the next chapters we'll talk about local directories like Google My Business that can help your business feature on search engines and other online resources.

We'll also talk about mobile, as local and mobile go hand in hand nowadays.

Local directories

If you're operating a physical store or provide services in a local area then you need to be listed on online local directories like Google My Business (www.google.com/business). Bing, Yahoo and other search engines also offer local directories.

To get started, just visit one of the local directories (you should probably start with Google as – like it or not – it's the most popular service on the Internet) and provide all the necessary info for your company like its business name, address, phone number etc. Proving the address also lets you add your business on online maps services like Google maps which is useful for people trying to get directions for your store or for those looking for certain types of businesses near them.

Make sure that you use the same business name on all online directories to avoid confusion.

You can easily add contact details like address, phone number and website on Google My Business.

Apart from the local directories mentioned above, there are also industry-specific directories (e.g. websites that list only local plumbers and electricians), review sites and apps like Yelp and Foursquare, and groups or pages on social media that might be relevant to the type of service you provide (e.g. Facebook pages about gardening and landscaping if you have this type of business). It's worth exploring where your competitors show up when you search for them on search engines and try to include your company on the same directories and websites.

Sometimes directories might ask for some kind of proof that you are, in fact, the owner of the business you claim to be. The process is usually straightforward and it's there to protect you from people who might want to pretend they own a business that it's not theirs.

Your company will probably make changes along the way so remember to update your online listings when necessary.

Location-based advertising

Online directories and review sites have replaced the phone book and are a great way for your business to be featured locally.

If you want to increase the chances of being noticed by an audience in your area you can also use local ads.

Google, Bing, Facebook, Twitter and most websites have a global scope. This means that if you're a business that serves only a particular area, showing up on a search on the other side of the world is not going to bring you customers.

And that's where the strength of local advertising lies in; it shows ads only to people who are near you and, thus, are potential customers.

Search engines, local directories, social media, review sites, all give you the ability of targeting people in a specific area.

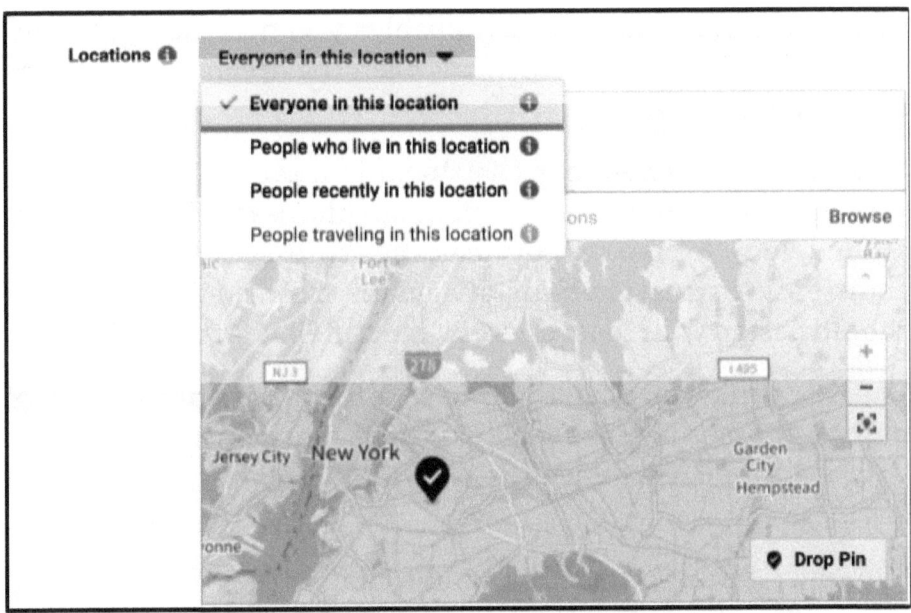

Facebook lets you target people in your area and specify the type of people that you are targeting.

For example, when you bid for a keyword on Google Ads you can restrict the area of the ad being shown on a radius of, let's say, 15 miles of the address of your business.

Social networks like LinkedIn and Facebook have similar targeting functionalities and you can use even a small budget to reach a sizeable amount of people in your area.

On review sites, you can usually pay to be featured on premium locations on the website, like for example when someone performs a search.

Local ads also enable you to make the ad more personalized by showing a different message to people near your shop, or by showing your ad only when you're open etc. You can use local ads to promote offers that are near you to lure them into your shop, help them by providing them with directions on their smartphone or letting them call you with a single tap.

The power of digital is that it enables you find the right audience at the right time, which has been the dream of marketers for decades.

What is more, remember that local is intertwined with mobile these days. People use their smartphones to find their way around, look for nearby services and stores, get recommendations etc. A smartphone is always in their pockets and you should design your local strategy around that fact.

The first thing you need to do to take advantage of the reign of mobile devices is make sure you have a responsive design for your website, i.e. your website should look good on all types of devices.

Moreover, your contact info and a map of your store should feature in a prominent position on your website as well as on local directories, your social media page and other relevant websites.

Websites and apps on mobile devices can use the GPS functionality to help users navigate – as long as the user gives the necessary permissions to apps to do this. This means you can detect people nearby and send them notifications through an app. For example, you can message people who are near your store with a special offer only for them. That's a great incentive for people to get them to visit your store.

As we mentioned previously, local advertising (on search engines, social media etc) is an excellent way to target only people who are in the local area (you can even limit this only during your opening hours), thus maximizing your chances of getting customers.

For example, if you have a barber shop you can limit your ads to people searching for haircuts or barber shops within a 20-mile radius of your business. Compare this to a generic ad that you'd place on the radio, TV, print or a news website. Which one is more likely to get you potential customers? Without dismissing the value of traditional media, digital marketing can help you find the people with the highest intent to buy your service and in the area that you can serve.

On TV or radio, as effective and popular as they might be, you can't control the limits of the broadcast (even a local station will probably show your ad to areas that you can't serve) nor can you target only people who are interested in your service. Thus, on traditional media you show your ad to as many people as possible, hoping that amongst them there will be a small portion that will buy your product – without, however, knowing if and when you actually influenced someone.

With TV, radio and print you just hope for the best. Digital advertising, on the other hand, will cherry-pick those people who are in the geographical vicinity of your store and are really interested in what you're selling.

Local search

Search engines can be very helpful for the discovery of your local business. In many cases, search engines will prioritize local businesses for particular searches, e.g. if someone is looking for a service in their area or if they are near a business offering what they're interested in.

So, how do you optimize your SEO so that you show up for relevant searches in your area?

First, you'll have to help search engines a little by letting them know where you're based at. Make sure your website includes all the info necessary like address, phone number, working hours, which areas you serve etc.

Your content is also a powerful indicator of location for search engines. For example, if you run a music store your blog could include info about gigs in your area or events that are of interest to musicians that take place in your store or nearby. Or you might have articles about local musicians including pictures and videos.

Offers for locals or people in the area are also a great way to attract attention from a local audience so make sure you include those in your content whenever possible.

Search engines are able to identify local content and thus, your website will be more relevant to people searching for the services you offer in your local area.

As we mentioned above remember to list your business on Yahoo! Local, Google My Business and Bing Local so that it's easier for search engines to find your business in your area.

Most users will be using their smartphone to search for a local business, especially if they're on the go, so it's important that your website is optimized for mobile devices.

SOCIAL MEDIA

Social media fundamentals

Social media are an integral part of our daily lives and an opportunity for businesses. Social media enable you to interact with your customers or people who are potential customers and reach far more people than other types of media.

Suppose you own a shop that rents and sells Halloween suits, superhero suits etc. People who rent your suits might be talking about your shop on social media already and maybe you can also post pictures of your new suits. This sparks conversation with your audience and creates awareness for your business.

Moreover, people can write reviews and comments about your shop spreading the word and building trust for your business. And of course, you can learn a lot by watching how people interact with your brand online.

A great video or piece of content can be shared thousand of times by people online. See what people like and share it on social media more often.

To start on social media, you need to create profiles on the big ones: Facebook, Instagram, Twitter, Snapchat, YouTube, Pinterest. You don't need to have accounts on all of the above; you can start with only one and see if it makes sense to add more on the way. There are more social media, of course, but it's better to start with the ones that have the largest audiences.

Try to have some activity (posting now and then) in order to grow your fanbase. Keep in mind that there are two types of posts on social media: ads and organic posts. We'll talk about ads later. When it comes to organic posts try not to be too salesy. People see social media as a place to hang out, so they usually appreciate if you treat the medium as a conversation for your organic posts.

Paid ads can be very effective for fulfilling your business goals, but we'll talk about them later.

You can start gaining followers by asking your existing customers to follow you on Facebook, YouTube etc. If you have valuable content their friends will follow and more people will spread the word for you.

Which social networks should you choose?

Social media like Facebook, Twitter, LinkedIn have now become daily terms that everyone knows. They are omnipresent and billions of people have accounts on them.

This means that if you're a business your potential customers are probably on those networks, so you should have some activity on the big social media.

However, there are some smaller niche networks that might be beneficial for your business.

For example, TripAdvisor for travel, or Opentable ad Four-Square for restaurants.

A membership and ads on those sites might reach fewer people than on Facebook, but you are reaching exactly the kind of customers you want to influence.

Also, pay attention to the purpose of each social network.

Some of them are personal, which means people use them to keep in touch with their friends and family. Of course, you can participate as a business, but you have to be careful not to overstep your boundaries. Your content should probably feel less salesy. Try to have a light, friendly and fun tone. Content that is interesting and provides useful information is always welcome by users.

Content-sharing networks, like YouTube, have more space to feature facts about the business and the products. Attention span on Facebook, for example, is far less than on YouTube.

Professional networks (think LinkedIn) connect people who want to find jobs or hire people or network with other professionals. Remember that LinkedIn is a good place to sell B2B services but not consumer goods.

When you start on social media, post organic content and connect with people. See how they respond to it. Don't jump into advertising right away but remember that this is a valuable marketing tool as well.

Social media goals

As in all things digital marketing, you need to start with your goals for social media. And those goals should align with your business goals.

First, ask yourself, what are you hoping to achieve by using social media?

Maybe you want to connect with your customers and potential customers and respond faster to their questions. Maybe you want to make people more loyal to your brand so that they become repeat purchasers. Or you want to expand your customer base to a new audience.

Let's say you have a goth-style clothes shop. In order to get more people to visit your store you want to raise some awareness about your business.

This is your first goal and will help you lay out your strategy.

First, you'll need to stand out from the crowd (goth clothes are a good start) and also find the audience you want to impress..

So, you can start with some Facebook or Twitter posts showcasing your new line of clothes or creating a Facebook event about the grand opening of your store.

Share your content with friends and family and encourage them to share it with their friends.

But don't be selfish on social media. Share your fans' content as well and other posts you think are relevant to your business. Or comment on other people's posts giving tips on their style, discuss some goth fashion trend or like a celebrity's goth look photos.

Also, you have to decide on your tone-of-voice for each social network. On LinkedIn you probably want to be more professional as you'll probably connect with suppliers or other companies.

Facebook is more playful and Instagram is all about visuals. Don't try to be someone you're not; for example, don't feel the urge to be funny and post memes if your business is a funeral parlor. Every business should have their own unique identity. Moreover, show your gratitude for people following your profiles and pages on social media. Those people are some of the most valuable customers you can have and they can be evangelists for your company. In many cases, their word is worth multiple times what an ad can do for you.

Moreover, you can create a mid-to-long term social media plan. This will include what content you will post, how regularly, specific events you want to include, and who you are targeting.

This is important because first of all you don't have time to just write spontaneous posts. You're focusing on your business so it'll be hard to find the time to write content if you don't have a plan.

A plan will help you know in advance what content you need to have ready and when.

Create a calendar with important topics and dates for your content. Are celebrations like Christmas and Diwali important for your business? Do you sell relevant items or do you expect increased business on those dates?

Moreover, what about your regular posting? Do you have to post every day or just once a week? More importantly, if you do post with a high frequency do you really have something new every time you post? Is it important or do you end up alienating and annoying your audience?

Once again, the posts should serve your business goals. If you're posting just because it's fun, you don't have to use your business profile; your personal profile is enough.

But if the content you're sharing makes people see the value in your brand, it convinces them to buy from your store, it helps them and builds trust in your company, then you're on the right path.

What is more, if you create your content in advance you can schedule to post it on later dates with tools like Hootsuite or Everypost. Those tools can cross-post on different social networks and automatically post them on the dates that you want. Also, you can take advantage of what is called social listening, i.e. monitor what people are saying about your business on social media.

Social media ads

As with search, social media also offer paid ads. And nowadays they are a powerful tool for many business in order to increase their sales and revenue.

Social media are not just a place to get likes and post cat videos anymore; businesses use them as any other advertising network where they can fulfill their business goals with the right targeting and message.

Going back to the beauty parlor example, let's say your customer demographic is usually women 18-45 within 10 miles from your store's location. You've been advertising on the local newspaper hoping to get this demographic to see your ad but you're not sure if they read the paper or not.

Wouldn't it be great if you can target only this audience?

Social media sites usually have this information about their users (gender, age, location, interests) as people usually add this info on their personal profile and they also indicate what they like by following pages, groups and interacting with posts.

So, in our example you can target women 18-45 in your store's vicinity and you can refine by interests like cosmetics, beauty etc.

As we said before you can start your social media presence with organic posts, but paid ads are a great way to accelerate this process. You can start with a small budget and reach a lot of people, which will usually have a lot more impact than an organic post, unless of course you are in the rare situation where your content becomes viral.

What's the main difference between search and social media advertising, you might ask. Let's take the two largest media Google and Facebook (which also owns Instagram).

People who know what they want to buy (they are in the intent phase) will search for something specific on Google. Search is also used by people who have been through the process of deciding that they need a product and they want to compare different brands or variations. This is especially true for expensive products as usually they are not impulsive purchases, but the customer will require a lot of information upfront before they make their mind.

So, products like flights, high-end electronics, expensive subscriptions are more suited for Google search and you'll usually find that this kind of companies spend the majority of their digital budget on Google rather than Facebook. Google search is also a great channel for purchases that happen only when the customer really needs it, e.g. plumbing services, doctors etc. You wouldn't be tempted to use a plumber if everything is fine in your house, just because you saw a great ad on TV or on Instagram.

On the other hand, Facebook and Instagram are very effective for inexpensive items, impulse buys and novelty items that you might not even know they exist. Facebook and Instagram are also very visual media, so creative (especially video) tends to be really important for your ads' performance.

Fashion items, cheap gadgets, apps, games usually perform really well on Facebook and Instagram.

It's also a great way to raise awareness for your brand and a cheaper alternative to TV ads for building your brand presence and reaching lots of people.

Keep in mind that most businesses will use their digital budget for multiple channels including search, social media, affiliates and others. It's important to know the differences between channels but also understand that you usually need a presence in at least the big ones.

Keeping track of social media goals

As in any other marketing activity, you have to use analytics tools in order to measure the effectiveness of social media on your overall marketing strategy.

First, social media themselves provide useful metrics. In the past, people would get obsessed about having a huge following and lots of likes for their business page and posts. Nowadays, companies have realized that likes and fans alone might not be a good metric to measure your success as a business.

Keep in mind that the ultimate goal for all your marketing activities should be to help achieve your business goals. Usually this means more revenue and higher return on investment. If a social network does not provide you with this kind of metrics you can use things like reach, clicks etc as proxy metrics.

But you have to be careful: just because you reached millions of people on a social network doesn't mean you're also convincing those people to buy your products.

When you become active on multiple social networks and channels in general you'll want to have a unified reporting and single source of truth. Analytics tools like Google Analytics or Adobe Analytics help you see where all your traffic is coming from.

This can be a starting point but it's not enough as different channels have different usage and functions. For example, Instagram is a visually-heavy network where a lot more impressions than clicks happen. On Google Analytics you would only see the clicks missing out on the impressions and a potential impact that Instagram can have on your branding and other activities.

To solve this social networks like Facebook provide incrementality testing (also known as lift tests) helping you understand the real impact of impressions and the whole activity on your business goals.

Moreover, analytics tools often provide attribution solutions. Attribution is the question of how we allocate the credit for a purchase to different channels, as they might all have been involved to convincing a user to buy from your store.

It is a complicated question and we're going to give more information on this in another chapter in this book.

Common mistakes on social media

The first rule of social media is that you are not the center of the universe. People use social networks to have fun, connect with friends, check the news etc. They're not there to see you standing on a soapbox trying to sell stuff.

Companies that use social media as a place to make a sales pitch are ignored and seen as boring.

So, if you have a beauty salon as mentioned before, you want to provide value to your followers. Merely posting your product pages on social media will alienate them. Instead, give them something valuable. For example, post how-to videos with beauty and make-up advice, or showcase beauty transformations and examples of innovative uses of certain products.

Moreover, social is not a one-way medium. People want to be heard too. Take advantage of social media by answering their questions, giving them tips and getting feedback.

Even negative feedback can be an opportunity for your company to show that you care about your customers and you're there even when things are tough.

If you don't intend to use a certain social network or if you don't have the time to update it regularly, it's better not to use it and instead focus on the networks that you can put an effort into keeping up to date. It's really weird to stumble upon a company page that has never been updated and feels like an abandoned old house.

Finally, always remember to measure your activity and efforts on social media. Use the social media and analytics tools to get a better picture on how you're performing and if you're engaging your audience.

THE WORLD IS MOBILE

Be mobile friendly

A lot has changed in the last decades when it comes to technology and especially mobile devices.

The first ever mobile phone call took place in 1973 and there was a commercial mobile phone available already in 1984.

The Motorola DynaTAC was the first commercially available mobile phone. It retailed for $3,995.

The evolution of mobile phones since then has been inconceivable. Smartphones have now fully fledged computing capabilities and adults spend more than 2 hours using them every day.

People no longer need to own computers. Instead they have access to the Internet, apps and software through their mobile phones.

What does this mean for your business?

Your marketing needs to reach people on where they spend their time, which is mobile devices.

The first thing to do is make sure your website is functional on mobile. Websites that render on all devices are usually called responsive, as they can adapt to the screen size and require-ments of each device.

Let's imagine you're an electrician that wants to expand your clientele. You can run an ad directing people to your website. Most people will use their mobile phone to visit your website.

A well-designed mobile website will feature your phone num-ber on top that can be tapped to make a phone call right away without the need for the user to scroll down to find your phone number.

What else can you do to make your site mobile-friendly?

Fonts and buttons should be easy to read and click on and the navigation should be easy and simple to use.

Moreover, your mobile site should be friendly to search engines as well. Mobile SEO is similar to regular SEO but it's important that on top of all other factors your site is user-friendly and loads fast.

Many people use mobile phones on 3G networks or slow WiFi so it's important that your site loads quickly. Make sure you com-press your images and remove any unecessary elements.

Google's Test My Site tool (https://www.thinkwithgoogle.com/feature/testmysite/) is a good way to test your site speed and get recommendations to make it faster.

Test My Site will test your site speed and give you recommendations on how to improve its performance.

Remember that people expect websites to load in less than 2 seconds in most cases. Any delay above that turns away potential customers. Thus, website performance is not just a nerdy tech issue but a business problem that you have to address.

Mobile apps

How do mobile apps differ from mobile websites? And should you create an app for your business?

A mobile site is usually a simpler version of your main site, made to work on a smaller screen. Mobile sites are accessed on a browser (Chrome, Firefox, Safari etc) whereas apps are downloaded on your phone.

Apps can provide functions that might not be easy to implement on a browsers, e.g. integration with GPS or a smartphone camera.

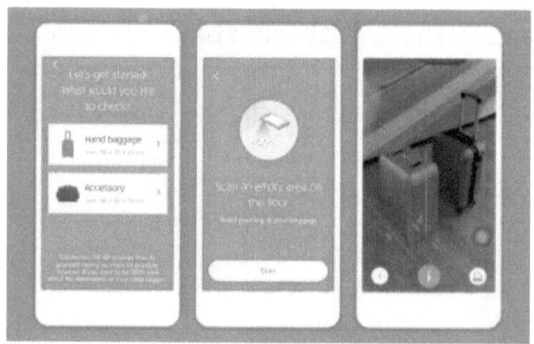

The Dutch airline KLM offers an app that helps users measure their suitcase's dimensions and see if it's within the limits allowed on flight. A great example of how an app offers functionality and value that a website couldn't.

Those feratures can be the reason why someone would install your app. If the app just replicates what a website could do there is no reason for the user to download the app.

Apps can boost your business if used in the right way. Let's say you own a movie theater and that you've decided to create an app that will help you sell more tickets.

Apps can send messages (or "push notifications" as they are also known) to a user's mobile phone even when the app is closed. You can send those messages whenever there is a new movie release or to announce special screenings and offers.

A benefit and reason for the user to use the app could be a loyalty program: every time they see a movie at your cinema they can use the app to earn points which can provide them with discounts at the concession stand or at the box office.

Moreover, the app can make ticket booking much easier saving time both for the user and your business. The GPS functionality can guide users to the cinema and your app could also send them reminders to be at the theater on time.

How do you start, then? First think if the app will provide any benefit to the user. If your app provides the same functionality as the website then there is no point in spending time and money developing it.

However, if you can provide extra value for the users and you can use your app to increase customer loyalty and return puchases then it's a good idea to have an app.

Start with your business goals and what actions you'd like your users to take on the app. The app space is cluttered so you might want to give them an incentive to get them use the app. Common benefits include discounts, loyalty programs, offers etc.

There are tools for building apps but you can always find a freelancer or agency to build an app for you. Websites like fiverr.com help you connect with professionals all over the world who can help you with tasks like building an app for a given budget.

Advertising on mobile

When it comes to your digital presence you should always think mobile first. This includes advertising, which can help you achieve different goals.

Mobile advertising gives you opportunities that you don't have on other devices. For example, you can target people on their location or get them to click on your ad and call you right away.

Your approach to mobile ads depends on your audience and your business goals. Remember that mobile behavior is different than usage of desktop computers. One main difference is that it's harder to type on mobiel devices. This impacts the way people use search engines as they will usually use shorter keywords and phrases to find something.

You should adjust your keywords to reflect this change on your mobile ads. Always think how you would use a search engine with a mobile device to determine if certain keywords make sense.

You can also use display ads for people visiting mobile websites. Mobile real estate is small so you need to present a compact but strong message within the confines of the mobile screen. Having a clear call to action is also crucial.

Mobile apps also offer advertising. For example, if you own a restaurant you can advertise it on the Yelp mobile app, so that people who are searching for restaurant reviews can come across your place.

Google Display Network and Facebook Audience Network can distribute your ad across thousands of websites and mobile apps.

You should also keep a few other considerations in mind. A good ad will bring people to your website. But you need to make sure that you have a mobile-friendly (responsive) website so that the precious traffic you acquired from the ad is not wasted.

Make sure you also use short text in your mobile ads and utilize ad extensions. Ad extensions are additional pieces of information like phone numbers or links for specific pages on your website.

Mobile search ads

Search ads can help you achieve your business goals, like getting more leads, phone calls or sales. The first thing to keep in mind is that your website is mobile-friendly.

Your loading speed should be really fast. People will just leave your website if it takes too long to load. Use Google's Test My Site (https://www.thinkwithgoogle.com/feature/testmysite/) to see your page's loading times and issues you could fix.

Moreover, test your website on different operating systems (iOS, Android, Windows Phone), different mobile devices (small and big screen sizes, older devices etc) and different networks (3G, 4G). You don't want to lose users just because you built your mobile website only with a particular device in mind.

Last, your website should be easy to use on mobile devices. Keep buttons big and easy to tap, avoid typing or minimize it if it's not entirely necessary and make navigation clear.

Search ads on mobile start with the keywords you're interested in - as with any type of search campaign. You could use the same keywords as your desktop campaigns but remember that typing is hard on mobile devices so people will use shorter phrases and keywords to search for something.

How can you figure out which keywords are popular on mobile devices? Start with Google Keyword Planner (https://ads.google.com/home/tools/keyword-planner/) to see search terms people are looking for and the percentage of those searches that come from mobile.

Compare the search terms that are more prominent on mobile vs desktop and you might see some interesting patterns.

Next, let's think about the ads. People are often interested on completing a task, e.g. there's a leak in their house and they need a plumber now!

That means that your ad should be focused to that task without the need for any other details. For example, if someone searches "leaking sink", show an ad that says that you can fix a leaking sink now. Don't mention that you can also fix their boiler, or install a new bathtub. This is irrelevant to them right now and probably annoying as they need to solve a very specific problem.

If you solve their specific problem now, rest assured that they will use your other services when they need them in the future. Timing is of the essence for search ads.

Now, a couple more tips on mobile ads. You can specify device preferences for Google search ads either as Mobile or All. Mobile preferred means that desktop users won't see your ads. That's a cool way to separate your mobile campaigns from desktop (or omni-device) ones if that's pertinent to the service you're selling as we saw in the example above.

Moreover, keep in mind that ad prices will differ on mobile and desktop for the same ad, as people behave differently on different devices. There in no rule of thumb here as this depends on the product you're selling, so you need to pay attention to your analytics and make adjustments to your bids.

For example, you might notice that people on desktop are much more likely to buy something from your e-shop than people on mobile. Let's say that the data shows that the conversion rate on desktop devices (how many people buy something out of all people who visit your site) who come from search ads is 20% higher than your mobile conversion rate for search ads.

This means you can use a bid adjustment to lower your price by 20% when your ads are shown on mobile devices. Bid adjustments can help you spend your ad budget more effectively

Mobile display ads

While search ads try to find people who are in the last steps of the marketing funnel (people who are almost ready to buy something), display ads try to capture people's attention before they have formed an intent to purchase your product.

The considerations for mobile ads also apply to display campaigns. Size is the first factor to think about. There are several screen sizes and resolutions so you have to design different ads for tablet and mobile devices.

You need to experiment and see what works on tablet devices which have bigger screen sizes and mobile phones.

If you're using Google Ads, you can take advantage of the Google Ad Gallery (https://support.google.com/google-ads/answer/156868?hl=en) to create ads for differnet formats and sizes.

You can also show your ads on mobile apps. You can choose which apps or types of apps to target so that they are relevant to the audience that can be your potential customers.

So, for example, if you have a cosmetics ecom shop you can show your ads on apps about beauty and healthcare.

There are several display networks like Google Ads, Facebook Audience Network and inMobi. All of them will enable you to show your ads on thousands of websites and mobile apps.

Mobile social media ads

Social media like Facebook and Instagram have billions of users and are great platforms for promoting your business.

As we've noted before decide which social media are more suited to your business. If you're a business-to-business company LinkedIn is probably the best option for you, whereas Instagram is great for fashion brands and Pinterest is where people search for design ideas.

Audience targeting is one of the major advantages that you can get by advertising on social media. You can target locations, demographics (age and gender), interests (e.g. people who like basketball) and other criteria like device or browser.

For example, if you're promoting your new iPhone app you can target only iOS users to make sure that only people with an iPhone will see your ad.

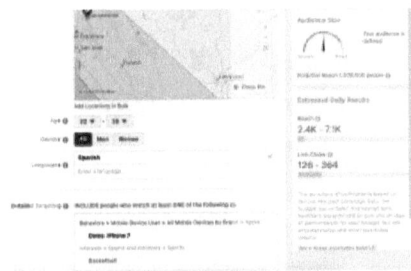

Facebook gives you a slew of option when it comes to targeting including interests, location, age, gender etc. It will also give you an estimate of the audience size and the daily results you'll get according to your budget.

Finally, make sure that your ad creatives are formatted for mobile. Use square or vertical pictures instead of landscape ones, make sure that the text and image are visible and that your message is optimized for mobile.

Video is a great way to stop people's thumbs when they scroll social media but you have to take into account a few design considerations. The duration shouldn't be too long; the rule of thumb says that a video ad for social media should not exceed 30 seconds, it should ideally tell the whole story in 10 seconds and should capture the user's attention within the first 3 seconds. Users browse content pretty fast on social media on mobile devices, so make sure your brand and message are visible from the get-go.

Video and image should be the primary formats to use on social media and not text. There are formats like carousel ads which can showcase multiple products to help you show more to your users.

Mobile video

Video is probably the most engaging way to capture the users' attention. Video is seeing a massive growth on mobile as WiFi- and mobile network speeds nowadays allow for fast transfer of data.

Video creation and distribution has been democratized. It's not necessary to have a huge production budget or to hire an agency to create a video for you. High-quality videos can be recorded on your mobile and there are countless video editing tools that you can use for free. Apps like iMovie, Quik, Splice and others can be used on your phone to edit videos and you can also upload your video right away on social media or other platforms.

When you create a video keep the following things in mind. First, make it relevant to your users. Create content that is helpful and interesting for them.

As mentioned before keep it brief and to the point. Attention spans on mobile are limited and people will makea decision on if they want to watch a video in 3 seconds. That means that the first 3 seconds of your video should be catchy and express clearly the message you want to convey.

Finally, make sure you have a clear call to action. Tell your audience explicitly and clearly what you'd like them to do after they've watched the video.

Let's say you have a beauty salon. You can create a video that demonstrates the skill of your make-up artists with before and after transformations. This is both interesting and showcases your services.

Upload your video and target it to the right audience. This could probably be people who live in your salon's vicinity and people who are interested in beauty and make-up.

For example, if you're advertising on YouTube you can choose to have your video shown as an ad on beauty and healthcare videos. That way you can reach people who you know are interested to this kind of services.

Moreover, you can target specific keywords and even websites and apps where you want your video add to show.

CONTENT MARKETING

What is content marketing

The Internet is based on the idea of creating and sharing content. This is the main reason why users browse the web and that's why good content can help your company stand out from the crowd.

Content includes blog posts, social media posts, videos and other types of material. The purpose of content marketing is to generate interesting, entertaining or helpful content so that it captures people's - limited - attention.

Good content marketing can boost your brand recognition, direct people to your website, improve your overall SEO and build a positive sentiment for your company.

Let's say you have a pet shop and you want to use content marketing to drive people to your website as your paid search budget is limited. Since your potential customers love pets you can regularly publish engaging content about pets on your blog and use social media platforms to promote it to your audience and their friends.

Great content starts with putting yourself in the shoes of your audience. What are they interested in? What is their passion or their problems? How can you help them or entertain them?

You could, for example, create videos with tips on pet grooming and wellbeing, or post funny and cute pet photos.

A good content marketing campaign aims to achieve three things: 1) answering people's questions, 2) providing value, 3) make them want more of your content.

And now, a few tips to write engaging content and have a successful content strategy.

Know your audience. Get acquainted with their interests, what accounts they follow on social media and what they generally like.

As with all marketing strategies and formats you have to test and learn. Experiment with different types of content and see what resonates with your audience. This includes the topics, tone and formats of your content.

Test differnet platforms on which to post your content. Maybe your content is better suited to Pinterest rather than on Twitter, for example. Find out where your users hang out on the web and how they post on those platforms.

Speak in the language of your users. In most cases, this is a natural everyday tone. People can understand when you just copy and paste stock business content. Find your tone of voice and don't pretend to be someone you're not.

The great filmmaker Frank Capra once said that the cardinal sin in movie-making is dullness. The same goes for your content. Don't be boring and try to stand out. Don't just copy other people's content, catchphrases and headlines. Try to be unique and interesting. This includes your content, images and headlines.

We'll see the points above in more detail in the following pages.

Know your audience

The first thing to do before you start creating your content is think about your audience and know them better.

Audience segmentation comes in handy on improving your targeting and content. Instead of trying to target everyone you can divide your audience into groups of people based on characteristics and interests. Segmentation helps to identify the people who are most keen on using your products, which leads to a more effective way to connect with your potential customers.

Let's go back to the beauty salon example. One of your audiences could be people who want a better skin treatment, and another audience could be people who are interested in fancy make up.

After you've identified your audiences you can start creating content relevant to them. For people with sensitive skin you can create content that will give them tips on how to keep their skin moisturized, for example. For the make up aficionados, you can create content with amazing transformations using specific cosmetics.

Audience segmetation will also help you target the specific people who are interested in that type of content.

For example, if you have a new line of cosmetics, and your website analytics show that people who are interested in this type of products are women aged 18-25 you can target your content to that group.

Moreoever, you can observ customer behavior and use that information to optimize your overall marketing efforts. Now that you know the interests of a specific audience you can try and find out how often they use and buy cosmetics. What social platforms do they use? Do they have any other interests and hobbies? For example, you might find out that people who like cosmetics also follow certain pop stars or browse the same websites.

All the above information can help you create content that's more relevant to this audience.

Online tools like Answer the Public (https://answerthepublic.com/), Google Keyword Planner and Google Trends (https://trends.google.com) can help you get more insights on people's searches and questions. This can be a useful inspiration for coming up with content.

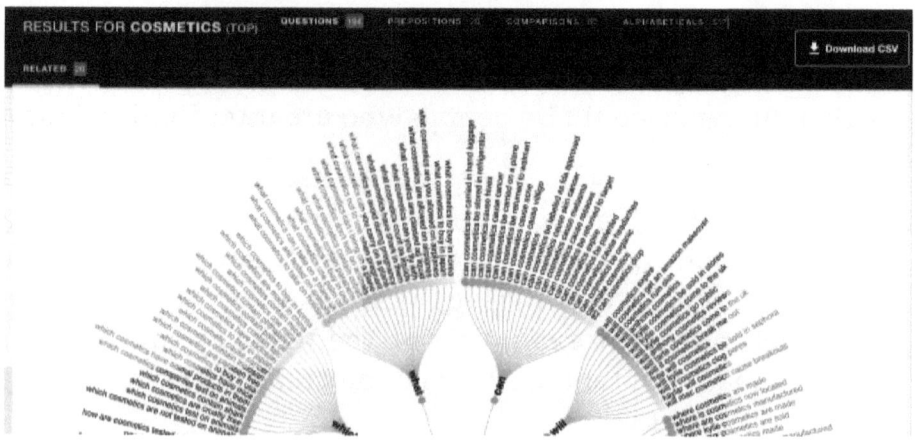

Answer the Public gives you a slew of information on what people are searching for based on keywords you provide.

What's more, social media platforms like Facebook and Twitter have their own analytics platforms which you can use to see people's behaviors, interests and demographics.

And as always, talk to real people. Ask your friends, customers and people who follow you online what questions they'd like to have answered and what is of interest in general.

Content format

Content ismuch more than just text on screen and can have many forms: images, videos, infographics, ebooks etc. Each format has different benefits and functions.

No matter what format you choose, the goal remains the same: to connect with your audience by helping them or entertaining them.

What types of formats are available for you to use?

Blogs are one of the most popular sections of websites and feature original content that can help increase awareness for your website and brand.

Infographics are a great way to present information in a visual way. They are eye-catching thanks to their aesthetics and the fact that they can present complicated content visually.

Ebooks are longer types of format. They usually are guides for a specific topic aimed to give readers practical content and can also make you establish yourself as an expert in your field.

Videos are really popular and can feature almost any type of content, from how-to videos, to unboxing or funny videos. It's one of the most engaging and entertaining ways for brands to draw attention.

The list of types of content does not end here. There are more formats like webinars, case studies and other formats depending on what kind of information you want to present to your audience.

Successful content is not necessarily viral content. By focusing on a niche audience and delivering specific content for them you can often get a lot more value as a business, as your potential customers can connect with your brand and move lower down the marketing funnel toward a specific action that you'd like them to take.

Moreover, think about the main goal of your content. Usually, there are four main purposes of content: to entertain, to inspire, to educate, and to convince.

Your content can serve one or more of those goals. Let's see an example on how to use different formats to fit to your goals.

Let's say you have a beauty salon. To entertain your audience, you decide to post a video of make-up fails on your social media profiles. To inspire, you plan to start a conversation on your social media where people can share their make-up stories and you can also answer their questions. To educate your audience, you can have a blog post written by a guest make-up artist with tips on how to apply certain make-up techniques and products. To convince people to come to your salon, you will share testimonials and reviews from happy customers and an ebook with secrets to the perfect make-up.

Consider how you can use content formats to match your content goals. Remember that content should always provide value to the user and not feel forced. You want people to develop a relationship with your brand as a result of you giving them content that makes their online experience better.

How to write content for the web

Content writing for online audiences is not exactly the same as writing offline content. There are some key differences and considerations to keep in mind.

The way we read and consume content is different online and offline. Elements like style, length and structure can have an impact on how to write for different media.

For example, users might have an adequate attention span to read a lengthy article in a newspaper, but they might abandon an article of similar length on a website.

Countless media and channels compete for our limited attention and time online, so we respond to shorter bits of content on the web.

Now, here's a few tips on how to write more effective online content. First, start with a catchy hook that explains to the user what they're about to read. Statistics, questions and lists seem to work effectively on setting up the right expectations for the reader.

As we've mentioned before always write with your target audience in mind. The content piece should offer them some kind of value. Put yourself in your audience's shoes; instead of trying to sell them something, try to help them, educate them or entertain them.

However, that doesn't mean that your content cannot lead to an action that you'd like your reader to take. As a matter of fact, you should include a call to action (CTA) to convince your audience to do something that aligns with your business goals. For example, it could be something like "sign up for our newsletter", "download your free ebook", "claim offer X" etc.

Coming up with ideas for fresh content can be challenging, but there are ways to get inspired and stay relevant to your audience.

You don't need to reinvent the wheel. Take a look at your competitors' sites and social media to see what kind of topics they're posting about. Make a list of the most popular topics and keywords and use them as a starting point for your content.

I've already mentioned tools like Google Keyword Planner and Answer the Public which can help you see relevant searches to the keywords you're interested in. Those are great ways to expand or refine your list.

Finally, make sure that you have a consistent and distinctive tone of voice and writing style. Whenever users read your content they can identify that it's you (the brand) that's talking to them, as if it was a person's voice.

This will help to boost your brand identity and awareness. It's important that you stand out from the crowd and that people can tell it's you. Your tone of voice should be in line with what your brand is trying to represent.

How to promote your content

It'd be a shame if all the time and effort you put into creating great content is wasted because no one reads your blog posts or watches your videos.

With so much competition online, it's essential that you promote your content in order to reach your audience.

Let's say you've created amazing content for your beauty salon. The first step to promoting your content is to understand where your audience spends their time online.

Do they use Facebook, Instagram or Twitter as their primary social network? Do they watch lengthy videos on YouTube or prefer to read blog posts?

For your content promotion plan you can group your channels into three categories: owned, earned and paid.

Owned are all the channels that are directly managed by you, like your website, blog or docial media profiles. These channels are free to promote on and they can be a great way to start your promotion if you don't have a big marketing budget.

Earned channels are channels that you don't manage yourself but someone else owns and they decide to share your content. For example, someone else's blog or social media account might share your content because they found it great. When something like this happens apart from the increased awareness and extra reach for your content you might see additional side-benefits like improved SEO thanks to other websites linking to your content.

Finally, paid channels are the ones that you have to pay for in order to promote your content. For example, you can boost your posts on Facebook to reach more people. Facebook will treat this as any other ad on their platform. You can select the people that you'd like to target who you believe are the ones that would probably find your content relevant.

After deciding which channels to use, it's a good idea to create a content calendar. A content calendar outlines the planned activity for creating and posting content for the next 3-12 months. By knowing what to post and when, can help you maintain a regular cadence of content promotion and it can make the content ideation easier.

Some things to consider for creating a great a content calendar:

- Be realistic. If it takes you a week to write, shoot and edit a video then it's probably not a good idea to include a new video on every day of your calendar. If the calendar is not achievable it's going to fail and you'll be disappointed.

- Highlight key dates. If Halloween and Mother's Day are important dates for your business then highlight them on the calendar and plan content around them. In general, have content planned for all the big holidays and seasonal events.

- Take into account all the channels you can use. Try to take advantage of synergies between different channels, like your blog and social media to promote your content.

- Keep your audience in mind. You don't have to reach everyone all the time. Segment your audience and specify which segments you'll target on each date of the calendar.

- Use tools to make your life easier. There are free and paid online tools that you can use to create a calendar and collaborate with other members of your team. You can even automate your content posting and other workflows.

How to track performance for content marketing

In order to know if your content marketing is delivering results, it's essential that you track your goals and regularly review them.

The first thing you need to do is define your goals and objectives and make them quantifiable and trackable. For example, you want to incrase the followers of your social media profiles by 50% within 3 months or you'd like to have 10 thousand pageviews on your website every month.

Content marketing should be tracked like any other marketing activity that can contribute to your business goals, be it sales, leads or any other goal.

Thus, you need to define the metrics that are important for your content's performance. This could be the traffic (sessions or pageviews) that your website receives from content on your social media, the sessions on your blog etc.

You should be watching these metrics overtime to see how your content is performing on a month over month or year over year basis. Past results are a good benchmark for you in order to improve your content.

You should take advantage of the free tools that social media platforms give you, e.g. Facebook Page Insights, to monitor your page's activity and information about your followers.

Facebook Page Insights provides you with info on your page posts, followers and other data that you can use to optimize your content.

You should also avail of free analytics tools - the most popular of which is Google Analytics - to monitor the behavior of people on your website, the most popular articles and pages and the journeys that people take to reach certain pages.

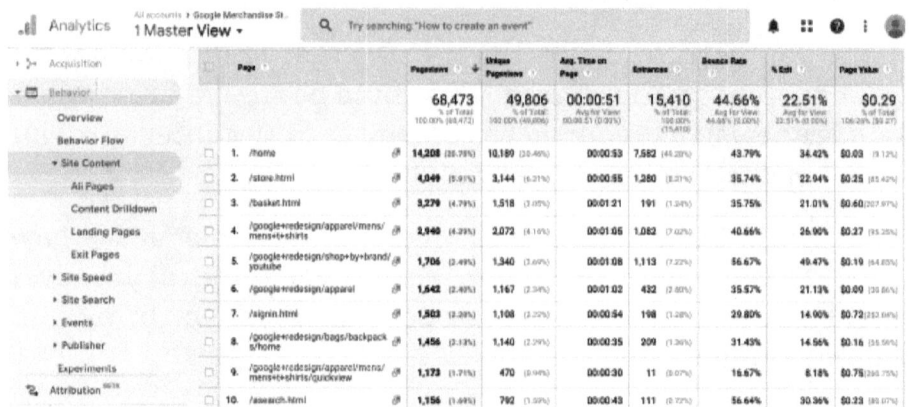

The report "All Pages" under Site Content in Google Analytics shows you the most visited pages on your website.

Your Google Analytics reports can reveal which articles and blog posts get the most visits or which ones people spend most of the time on. This data can help you understand which topics are more popular and you can use that information to modify your content plan so that it includes more of those topics.

Analytics tools can also show where readers come from, e.g. social media or a search engine and how many of the people who read your content buy something from your site after watching a video or reading an article on your blog. This could help you quantify the value of content for your overall marketing plan and also make adjustments to your content strategy.

EMAIL MARKETING

Intro to email marketing

Email marketing has been one of the most effective forms of digital marketing since the early days of the web. It is cost-effective and can build customer loyalty.

As with all marketing activities, first you need to set your goals. How do you intend to use email marketing?

Are you going to be sending newsletters about your products and services, to drive traffic to your website? Do you want to increase your sales by sending out offers and vouchers?

Email marketing requires a list of people who have given you their email address and are interested in your business. How do you build that list of emails?

Whenever you have an interaction with customers offer to send offers if they give you their email address. On your website you can have a form with a clear call-to-action to subscribe to your newsletter and state what benefits they get if they do.

Make sure that you comply with all privacy-related laws like GDPR in the European Union and that people give you their permission to receive emails when they sign up for the newsletter.

Now that you have a list of people who would like to receive emails from your company, you have to keep a few things in mind.

First, don't flood people with constant emails or even emails that have too much content. Keep your content brief and to the point and always start with a friendly introduction. If you have lots of different products you can ask people a couple of questions to segment them and send more relevant emails in the future.

Then, you can send offers for the specific products they're interested in and content that is relevant to their interests.

You can also use your email to get more info about your customers. Ask them about their interests and if they'd like to receive offers about other products as well. Moreover, try to find out what their preferred channels and means of communication are.

Ask them for example, if they'd like to receive emails on a monthly or weekly basis and record all the above information in your database.

Email marketing is a great tool for people who have been customers for a long time. Send them relevant info to their product they've purchased even if it was a long time ago and try to rekindle your relationship with them by sending an offer.

Not all email communication has to be offers and vouchers. Sending entertaining or educational content from time to time helps build a positive sentiment towards your brands. If your content is outstanding it will make people anticipate your next newsletter.

What's more you can use email to get feedback on your company and products. It's a good idea to respond to them directly if you have the capacity. People like to know their feedback is being heard.

Always thank them for being a customer and offer a solution to their issues.

Email is a great way to interact with your customers and as long as you have that list of emails, it's virtually free to send to your contacts.

Email marketing basics

The easiest way to get started with email marketing is an email marketing service, e.g. Mailchimp. An email marketing service will feature a contact database that stores info like email addresses and names of your customers.

You can import the customer data you already have to your marketing service.

Email services will also provide the ability for users to subscribe and unsubscribe. This is usually done through a form that you can add to your website. Whenever a user submits their email through this form, their data is automatically added to your contact database.

These forms can be customized to match the style of your website. Also, remember that sign up forms should be as short as possible. If you ask too much information from your users it's less likely they will sign up. Usually, just their email is enough for subscribing to your newsletter.

You can use other info you have about your clients to create sub-lists of your database. For example, if you have a sports equipment store and you know the sports that people play you can divide them into different lists for soccer, basketball, skiing etc. Then you can send different newsletters to every list with products that are relevant to the sport they like.

The next step is to think about the emails you're going to send. Email marketing services have templates that you can use and tweak so that you make a recognizable email for your brand that you can use over and over.

Make sure that your email is mobile-friendly as many people will read your email on their smartphone. You can preview and test your email before you actually send it out.

Another feature that you can take advantage of is the fact that you can schedule when your emails are sent out. You can track the days and times when people most often open your email and decide to schedule sending your emails at those times.

Your emails will most likely include some links, e.g. links to the products on your website. You can also track if people click on those links and what they do after they visit your website. For example, you might want to see the percentage of people who buy something on your website after they've clicked on a link your email (also known as conversion rate).

Observing and tracking these behaviors can help you optimize your email content in the future.

You can even personalize email content based on a person's interests. Using this feature that email marketing services offer you can send tailored messages to different people on your contact database.

Personalized messages usually have better email open rates and can increase your chances of people going to your website and even making a purchase.

How to create successful emails

Sending the email through your email marketing service is the first step. The next one is to grab people's attention, make them open your email, read it and take the actions that you want them to take.

Le's say you're sending an email for your beauty salon. How do you convince people to open it and read the content?

The first thing that people see in their email inbox is the business name in the "From" field and the subject of your email.

The "From" field should clearly identify your company/brand. People will be wary of emails sent from people or organizations they don't recognize.

The subject line is your chance to convince people to open your email. Internet users receive dozens of emails and newsletters in their inbox every day - so how do you stand out?

Your subject line should be short (under 10 words) and clear. It should highlight the most important piece of information in the email.

Email marketing services provide you with the ability personalize newsletters by including info like the recipient's name, e.g. "Anna, have you heard of the latest makeup trends?".

Remember that words like "free", "bargain", "$$$", exclampation points usually trigger spam filters so make sure you avoid them.

After your users have opened the email you want them to read the content and take some kind of action. Users have a short attention span so they will skim your message. That means your content has to be as brief as possible to convey the message that you want.

Avoid lengthy paragraphs and sentences and include links. Links should ideally feature calls to action that encourage users to take an action like click to go to your website.

Calls to action should give an incentive to the reader to click on them, e.g. "click here to avail of a 50% discount".

Use formatted text (bold, italics, underlined) to make important content stand out.

At the bottom of the email you'll have to include a few more things. Those include links so that the users can unsubscribe, change their email preferences or update their contact information.

This is usually required by law and the lack of those options result in a bad experience for your users, so don't try to hide them.

Email marketing campaigns

One of the most effective methods for creating successful email marketing campaigns is A/B testing.

With A/B testing, you create two versions of an email and see which one performs better.

For example, let's say you're sending an email about your new products. Which subject line should you use to catch people's attention? You can create two versions of your email, one with subject line A and one with subject line B. The email itself is exactly the same in both versions but the only difference is the subject line.

Half of your contacts list will receive version A and the other half version B. Then, after you've sent the emails you compare the open rates for both versions, i.e. what percentage of people open each subject line. The one with the higher open rate is the winner of the test and that means you've gained some valuable insights on how to craft a better subject line next time you send an email.

You can test various elements such as subject lines, content, images, formatting, frequenct of sending emails etc. For example, you can see the difference between sending emails during lunchtime and in the eveneing. Or what happens when you send version A on Monday and version B on Friday.

Keep in mind that, ideally, you want to test one element every time you perform an A/B test. So, try not to test a different subject line, content, image and frequency at thte same time. The reason is that when the test ends and you have a winner you don't know which of the elements was the deciding factor.

Moreover, make sure you have enough recipients to perform a test and that the metric you're using to determine the winner of the test is significant for your business. Usually, the metrics you want to focus on are open rates, click-through-rates (how many people click on the links of the email to go to your website) and conversion rates (how many people bought something from your website coming from an email).

Your email campaigns will often lead people to specific landing pages and not just the generic homepage of your website. If, for example, you're sending an email about a new offer only for the recipients of the newsletter, then an offer-specific landing page should be created for that purpose.

Finally, make sure your email and landing page work well across all devices. Don't forget to track your email campaigns' performance.

Email marketing services include analytics tools that can show you how well your campaigns perform.

By gathering data you can identify patterns on which subject lines are more compelling, or which type of content drives more traffic to your website. Pay attention to the reports and use the data to optimize your campaigns over time.

Email metrics to track

In order to measure the effectiveness of your email marketing activity you need to pick the right metrics to track.

Open rate is the ratio of people who opened the email out of everyone who received your email. This mainly shows how effective your subject line is. This is the main metric to use for an A/B test where the only difference between the two versions would be the subject line. As you gather more and more data points on this metric you will be able to craft successful email subject lines.

The next metric to look into is Click Through Rate (CTR). This shows how many people clicked on one of the links in the email as a percentage of all people who opened the email.

Another metric to focus on is Conversion Rate. A conversion is athe action that you ultimately want people to take on your website. Usually this is a purchase but in cases where people cannot buy items on your webstie it might be a lead (e.g. completing a sign up form), registering for an event etc.

Conversion rate is simply the number of people who made a conversion divided by all the people who received the email.

Last, it is important to know if your email actually reached your users' inbox. When an email is rejected we say it bounces. Bounce rate is an important metric to track and it's simply the ratio of emails which couldn't be delivered out of all the emails you sent.

Email marketing services will usually inform you about both soft and hard bounces. A soft bounce means that someone's inbox was full and couldn't receive any more emails at the time. A hard bounce means that someone has blocked your email address or that the email you have on your contact database is wrong.

Email addresses that lead to hard bounces can be removed from your contact list as they will not be able to receive your email.

Make sure you track the above metrics overtime to see if you are improving your performance when it comes to email marketing.

A campaign not measured is a campaign that you will never know if it was worth doing.

DISPLAY ADVERTISING

Display advertising basics

When you visit a website you will notice banner, text and video ads on the pages you browse. The first ever banner ad was published in 1994 and had a click-through-rate of 44% which is extraordinarily impressive for today's standards.

The first ever banner ad on the web was bought by AT&T on the website hotwired.com.

All these ads you see on various websites are called display ads. Display advertising is the web equivalent of billboards, print or TV ads. Websites sell part of their website real estate as ad space to businesses who hope their ads will be seen and clicked by website visitors.

A banner ad on cnn.com.

In order to run a display ad on a website you can make a deal directly with a website, say your local newspaper's website, or you can use ad networks that will display your ad on mulriple websites without you having to contact those websites. Moreover, ad networks will match your ad to the right websites so that you target the users most relevant to your product.

Some of the most popular ad networks are Google Display Network, Facebook Audience Network, AdRoll and others.

These networks give you the option to show your ad on specific websites and specific audiences.

For example, let's say you want to advertise your soccer jersey eshop. You can advertise on relevant websites like sports news sites, soccer tournament websites and soccer fans' forums.

But you can also target soccer fans when they visit other websites, since you can target people with specific interests no matter what the website they visit. Display ads are dynamic, i.e. they change every time a new user visits the website. Thus, the ad that I and you will see when we both visit the same website at the same time will be different if we have different interests.

Display ad networks will take care of this so the only choice you'll have to make is which audiences to target. Display advertising is a great way to build awareness for your brand and product as you can show your ad to tons of people on websites around the world.

Moreover, banned ads are clickable so you use display ads to drive traffic to your website. You can also choose to target people who have already visited your website. This is called retargeting and you can tailor your messages to those people since you know that they already know your business so you want to convince them to take the next step, e.g. subscribe to a newsletter or buy something.

We'll see the above in more detail in the following sections of the book.

Differences between search ads and display ads

The most popular forms of advertising on the Internet are search ads (also known as PPC or SEM) and display ads.

In this section of the book we'll look into differences between search ads and display ads.

Let's say you just read an article about the benefits of running so you decide to start running long distances. You think it's a good idea to buy some new running shoes so you visit Google and type "best shoes for marathon running".

This behavior means that you've made up your mind on what product you want and you are active in your search for finding it and possibly buying it.

Search ads are a great way fro companies to reach potential customers who are in the last stages of the marketing funnel and are actively looking for something.

Dispaly ads are different. The people who see your ads are not necessarily looking for your business or product. In fact, they might not even know your services or have thought about buying.

However, that fact doesn't render display ads useless. On the contrary, they can serve a very valuable role in your marketing strategy.

As with TV or print ads people are not always actively looking for your product when they encounter one of your display ads. But by targeting the right audience (e.g. placing your offline ad on the right magazines or billboard locations) you can reach people who might be interested in your business.

Since you can choose which websites to show your dispaly ads on or target specific audiences and interests you can expand your reach beyond the circle of people who already know they want to buy your product.

In the running shoes example, it might be people who are generally interested in sports or are track and field fans.

Also, keep in mind that search ads will only show up on the search engine and only for the specific keywords that your ad is associated with. So, if someone's left the search results page they won't see your ad elsewhere on the Internet.

Display ads, on the other hand, can show up on any website and app in the world that offers available advertising space. This means that people visiting news sites, blogs, entertainment sites and millions other websites can see your ad, if of course you've chosen to advertise on those websites.

Finally, search ads are made up of text as we've seen before. There is a headline, a text and a link. Display ads are much richer, giving you the ability to tap into different formats and sizes, including video and images. This means that display ads reward creativity as you can catch people's attention by creating great visuals and compelling ads.

Search ads and display ads might be different but they can work together to maximize your marketing efficiency. A display ad can be the introduction of your company to a user who might not even be aware of your existence. Later, when you've spread the word for your company and services the same user might use a search engine to search for a product that you're selling. If you're company shows up on the search results then you have good chances of turning the user into a paying customer.

A deeper look into display ads

Let's take a look at how to make display advertising more effective for your business.

As mentioned above, you're probably going to be using an advertising network like Google Display Network or AdRoll. That way you can advertise on multiple websites and target the right audience for you.

Display ad networks offer several targeting options like language, time and day for your ad to show up, device type, geography.

There is also the ability to advertise only on specific websites or specific pages of a website and even specific areas on those pages. In digital marketing parlance these are known as placements and you should be choosing websites and pages that are pertinent to your business and product.

However, there are instances when you might want to target a broaded audience, especially if you're not sure about who your average customer is and you want to increase your brand awareness and reach more people.

Instead of selecting specific websites you can select a category like "sports", "health and beauty" or "cinema" and let the ad network pick the right websites for you. Or you can target people with specific interests instead of websites. That way your audience will see the ad no matter what website they're browsing.

You can target people by age, gender, geography and interests based on their browsing behavior.

Of course, in order for your display marketing to work you will need captivating ads. Ad banners come in many different formats and sizes. You can even use video which is a great way to draw attention.

By creating different formats for the same ad you will maximize all the potential placements for your ad. Your creative should, of course, be relevant for your audience. An ad cannot be judged as good or bad on its own; it's how relevant it is with its audience that deems it successful or not.

In order to organize your display activity you will create campaigns which will contain your ads and targeting.

For example, if you have a sports store you can have a soccer campaign with multiple ads that target soccer lovers; one campaign for basketball fans and so on.

A campaign can include multiple ads and multiple audiences. Try to keep your campaigns organized by audience and name them in a consistent manner so it's easier for you to find what you're looking for when you end up having lots of different campaigns.

Display advertising goals

Before you start advertising on display you need to decide what your goal for this marketing activity is.

Are you going to make your brand known to people who are unaware of it? Say something to people who already know your company? Make customers loyal by bringing them back to your business so that they make more purchases?

Of course, display gives you the ability to do all of the above but you have to decide how display advertising fits into your marketing strategy.

Remember that you can create multiple campaigns for your display advertising. That helps you serve different goals if you're trying to achieve lots of different things with display marketing.

By deciding upfront what goals you'd like to achieve you can build different ads for different audiences.

In order to do this, think as a customer and try to figure out the journey that a real person would take in order to purchase something from your business.

First comes awareness. Let's revisit the sports store example. Before someone buys from your store they need to know that you exist. Display is ideal for reaching a broad audience; you'll, of course, need to create the right creatives for making a great first impression it. Always keep in mind that people are not searching for your business when they see your ad and they might not even be aware of what your company does.

Consider what can make your ad really stand out. Is a local team using gear from your sports store? Do you have any great fitness stories from your customers? Do you offer something unique as a store?

The next stage in the marketing funnel might be making people interested in your brand and ensuring they will remember you in the future. If this is one of your goals you can create ads that showcase your company's competitive advantages like low prices or great service.

Since you targeted a broad audience during the first phase of your display activity, you might want to narrow down your audience in phase two. For example, you can target people who have already visited your website or people with specific interests that match what you offer.

Next, you might want to move to the stage of the funnel known as consideration, i.e. people who are thinking of buying the product that you offer. Here you can showcase specific products in your ads and give more details about them, for example an ad showing the amazing new sneakers that your store is selling exclusively in your area.

This ad will be limited to a specific audience, namely people who've shown interest in your product but haven't bought it yet.

The final step in the customer journey is, of course, the purchase. Your goal as a business is to get people to buy your products and that should be reflected in your display ads, as well.

For this phase you could show ads with special offers or incentives for people to buy your product. Obviously, you'd be retargeting people who have shown interest in your product, e.g. people who have visited a specific product page on your website or people who added something to their online cart but didn't make the purchase.

Retargeting campaigns are usually the ones with the highest conversion rate as they show their ad only to people who have been really close to buying something.

So, defining your goals based on the customer journey can help you decide the kind of ads that you will create for every step of the funnel.

Display advertising networks

Display advertising networks are the middleman connecting businesses who want to advertise with websites that have ad space to sell. Some of the biggest advertising networks are Google Display Network, Facebook Audience Network, AdRoll and others.

Let's see how you can use them by using the sports store example. Let's say you have a sports website in mind that you think attracts potential customers for your store.

One way to advertise on that website would be to contact the site directly and work out an advertising deal. This can work if you want to advertise only on one website and if that website has the capacity to deal with all the advertisers who need its space.

However, with a plethora of websites and advertisers this can get complicated and time consuming. That's where advertising networks add value to this activity. They handle both the selling and buying of ads by connecting thousands or even millions of websites and advertisers.

Websites that have available ad space can sign up on these networks to sell that space. They can decide on the minimum price for the different placements on their site and let the advertising network fill the empty ad space for that price.

Your company can then bid for the placements that you're interested in. You have access to all the websites and their placements that are part of that advertising network and you can choose which websites you want to advertise on.

The buying and selling of an ad space on a specific page happens every single time a page is loaded. That means that if a certain page on a website is loaded a thousand times on a given day, a thousand auctions (buying of the ad space) will happen on that day. This also means that every user can potentially see a different ad on the same page based on several factors.

Each network decides those factors differently, but at their core they all have the same principle: they try to match buyers and sellers to fill all available ad spots.

Through ad networks you can target the audiences that you think are the most relevant to your business, either by targeting specific website categories or by targeting certain characteristics of the users. This way you'll get to show your ads to the right people according to the criteria you select.

What is more, advertising networks can help you manage your advertising budget. Since buying and selling of ads is dynamic and happens all the time, the network will collect the money from the advertisers and handle the payments to the websites.

Another importan feature of advertising networks is that they collect and provide data to companies on their network.

You'll get reports on how many times your ads were shown, how many clicks they generated, their cost, their targeting etc.

You can also track what happens on your website after someone's clicked on a display ad, e.g. if they made a purchase after seeing one of the ads on the display network.

Before you sign up for one of the advertising networks make sure to avail of anny of the introductory offers that they usually provide for signing up. Don't forget to test your ads and watch the reporting to see how they perform.

Retargeting

We've mentioned retargeting before, which is a form of advertising where you target people who've already visited your website or performed a certain action.

In our sports store example, a potential customer visits your webstie searching for a new pair of sneakers. They like the product and even add it to their online cart but for some reason they don't complete the purchase.

Although their visit and the fact they added something to cart shows that they have a strong intention of buying something from your company it's a shame that in the end they didn't actually make the purchase.

And although they were strongly thinking of buying that pair of sneakers at the time of their visit on your website, they might forget about it eventually or buy sneakers from a competitor of yours.

Enter retargeting. By targeting people who've already visited your website and defining the audience based on what action they took you can show them ads that are specific to what they did earlier on your site.

So, you could, for example, target all the people who added something to their cart but didn't complete the purchase. Or all the people who visited the "sneakers" category on your site but didn't buy anything.

This information is anonymized, i.e. you don't store anyone's emails, names or any other personally identifiable information. It's just a list of anonymized cookies that can be matched by your retargeting ads.

The ads that you will show to that audience can be very specific and focused since you know that these people are past the stage where they need to learn about your brand. They obviously already know your company, they visited your website and were doing or trying to do a specific action.

So you might give them an extra incentive to finalize that action, e.g. a voucher, an offer or a reminder about the product and how awesome it is.

This means that you can also exclude retargeting audiences from your generic (top of the funnel) brand awareness campaign. You can now spend your marketing budget more effectively as you dedicate a part of it for people who have visited your site before even after they've left it to show them very specific ads.

Your retargeting lists can be dynamically updated based on the actions users take. So you might have a retargeting list for people who've added something to cart without buying and an exclusion list for everyone who's bought something. As soon as a person who added something to cart buys something they're automatically moved to the latter list from the former one.

Retargeting is a very powerful tool which if used effectively can have a great return on investment for your marketing activities.

VIDEO

Video is everywhere

With the proliferation of fast Internet connections, online video is becoming omnipresent. Thus, video has become a valuable tool for online marketing.

Today, video is consumed on all types of devices and is used for education, entertainment, information, but also for advertising.

How can you incorporate video into your marketing strategy? There are platforms dedicated to sharing video like YouTube and Vimeo where you can upload your video creations and even embed them on your website.

These video services also give you the ability to run ads on other people's videos. And of course you can run video ads on social media and display ad networks.

Video is a great way to catch people's attentin and advances in technology have made it easier to produce video without breaking the bank.

Video as part of your marketing plan

Video can and should be an integral part of your online presence. Once again, we will start with your goals and how video can support them.

In order to optimize video for your strategy it's helpful to think what kind of content your customers consume and look for. Aligning your goals with your customers' needs and wants is an ideal way to plan your strategy.

For example, say you provide meal delivery kits to people. People submit their dietary needs and preferences and you deliver the ingredients once a week so they can cook their favorite meals.

Your customers will definitely be interested in recipes for different diets and needs, e.g. vegan or keto. You can create and share a video of how to make a great vegan dish. People will find the information they need and be exposed to your company at the same time.

Even if you don't have the time and resources to produce your own videos you could always avail of other people's videos and advertise on their content. For example, you could sponsor a cooking channel on YouTube or just advertise your webstie on cooking videos.

A static ad displaying as a banner on a YouTube video.

Video advertising enables you to select categories of videos or specific videos where you'd like your ads to appear. Your ads don't have to be videos themselves; they could appear as text or static image while the video is playing.

And of course you can choose if you'd like your ads to be clickable and direct people to your website.

Make videos without break-
ing the bank

Today it's easier and cheaper than ever to produce videos. Technogical advances in cameras (even the ones on your smart-pohne) and editing software have made video creation more accessible than ever.

As with any other type of content you should start by planning your video content. Planning helps you shoot many videos at the same time, especially in cases where your videos share the same location and resources. That will save you time and effort.

A good idea is to create a storyboard for your video before you shoot it. A storyboard is a visual outline of your video, showing what happens on every scene. You don't need to have great drawing skills to make a storyboard. Even stick figures and simple shapes can help someone understand what the video is about.

Storyboards don't need to be complicated, but will help you in planning your shots.

Next, you'll have to think about production. There are agencies that can create videos for you but you can also make your videos in-house to save money.

Your smartphone camera is more than enough in most cases and there are lots of editing tools that you can use. Some of them like iMovie or Shotcut can be used for free and there are a lot of mobile apps that you can use to edit your videos if you wish to do everything on your phone. Some of those apps are Splice, Quik and others.

Of course the cost of a video production is not limited to the camera and software so you can minimize your costs by using props that you or your friends have, asking a friend to take part in the video so that you don't have to hire an actor, and using locations like your home or office to shoot your video.

During filming there are a few things to keep in mind to make your video look "professional". A tripod is a sine qua non when it comes to creating a video that will not nauseate your viewers. An external microphone is a great addition if you want high quality sound as smartphone mics are rarely suitable for this kind of recording.

And lighting can make or break your picture quality regardless of how good your camera is. You don't necessarily need to buy any lighting equipment, but make sure your filming location is well lit.

Finally, when you have all your footage, use one of the editing tools to put the shots together, add music and maybe some effects. Editing tools have features that enable you to color-correct your movie and make it look prettier.

And of course, don't forget to have fun when creating your videos!

Make your videos be seen

If a tree falls in a forest and no one is there, did it make a noise? Even if you can't answer that philosophical question, when it comes to online video it is an undisputed fact that if you make a great video but no one watches it, it was a waste of time and resources.

Let's say you just completed your amazing makeup video for your beauty salon and you've uploaded it to YouTube and Vimeo. Make sure the title, keywords, tags and description are accurate and relevant to the content. This will help people find your video on search results when they use those keywords.

Moreover, accurate titles and descriptions manage the viewer's expectations. If the title is not representative of what the video is about, viewers will be dissapointed and they will not follow your channel. Moreover, they can upvote or downvote your videos which will have an impact on how they show up on search results.

Call to actions should be included in the videos. For example, you can ask viewers to share the video, visit your website to see your new offers or sign up for a newsletter.

Your videos don't have to live only on video hosting platforms like YouTube. You can embed them to your website and make sure you post videos often as part of your content plan.

If a video is not relevant anymore (e.g. a video that advertises an event that has already taken palces) you should remove it. Moreover, let your users know about your new videos through your social media channels and newsletters.

If you regularly produce quality video, your users will be expecting your new videos with a specific cadence.

Envourage your social media followers to share the videos you post on Facebook, Instagram and other social networks, and don't forget to use hashtags (e.g. #beauty, #makeup for your beauty salon) to improve your visibility on social media sites.

Ads on video platforms

Millions of people spend hours every day watching videos on sites like YouTube, DailyMotion or Vimeo. Since there are videos for any category you could think of, these sites are a great place for your business to advertise to people interested in your products.

First, start by defining your target audience and what kind of videos they would consume on sites like YouTube. If you own a beauty salon, then your potential customers probably watch videos about health, beauty and makeup.

Search for channels that produce content that is relevant to the interests of your audience. You can see how many followers a channel has and how many people have viewed each of their videos.

Now think about how you can talk to that audience. Do you have any makeup tutorials that users can find interesting and helpful? Do you have content with celebrity makeup artists visiting your shop and talking about their work? Or maybe info on new makeup products?

Your ads can be in different formats: video, text or image. You can even avail of tools like the ones included in Google Ads where you can take advantage of image libraries to create image-based ads.

Make sure to include a call to action and an incentive for users to visit your website, e.g. by featuring visually compelling content on your website or directing them to an offer page.

After selecting your audience and the format of your ad you can also choose the placement, i.e. where your ad will appear. For example, you can show it next to the video or in the video.

And as always set your KPIs (key performance indicators) based on your business goals and monitor them regularly to understand if your campaigns on video sites are effective as part of your overall marketing plan.

Measuring video

As we've noted multiple times in this book, every marketing activity should be measured. Video is a valuable part of your overall marketing strategy but you only know what it's really worth when you're measuring its effectiveness.

Video analytics can help you with information on your users including demographics and their location. By knowing your audience you can tailor your video content so that it's more interesting to them.

For example, say you own a company that sells diet plans. Your analytics shows that a big chunk of your users live in the Netherlands and that videos featuring gluten-free recipes are really popular.

By taking into account these insights you might want to create videos in Dutch and not just in English; and moreover increase the amount of content dedicated to gluten-free. Or even adjust your diet plans to include gluten-free options.

You might even find out that different platforms (e.g. YouTube, Vimeo, Facebook) reveal different behaviors about the people who use each one of them. Also, you know which of the platforms generate most of the views for your videos. That way you can focus on the channels that have the biggest followings and traffic for you.

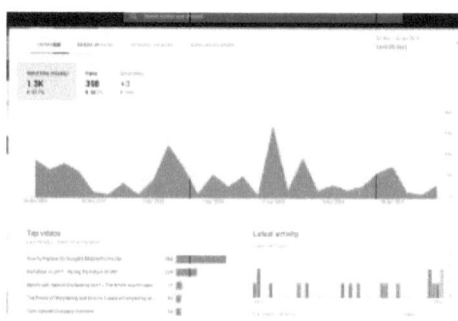

YouTube Analytics provides insights on your channel and videos.

You can also get reports and the times and days that people watch your videos. If you notice that most users watch your videos on Sunday afternoons, it's a good idea to upload your new video every Sunday morning.

Morevoer, you can find out if users watch the whole videos or just a part of them and for how long. In general, attention spans on the Internet are very short, so keeping your videos as short as possible ensures that people won't abandon the viewing.

If you notice that people watch only the first few seconds and then leave, it means that the video doesn't meet their expect-ations. Your title and description should reflect what the video is about. And remember that the first seconds are really crucial to keep someone watching, so make sure you start by explain-ing what the video is about and giving them an incentive to stay by making the intro impressive and unique.

The average length of video viewed can give you an indication of how long your videos should be. If the data shows that people watch 2 minutes on average, then try to make videos that match that length - or are even shorter.

Keep an eye on other metrics as well, such as likes, comments and shares. This shows if people interact with your content and how they perceive it, positively or negatively.

Sharing is the strongest sign of engagement, as it means that people are willing to spread the word for your video.

ANALYTICS

Intro to analytics

Analytics is the collection and use of data to generate insights for your business. Ideally, these insights will help you make better decisions in order to achieve your business goals.

Web analytics is based on collecting data from your website and there are a lot of tools that you can use such as Google Analytics, Adobe Analytics, Kissmetrics and others.

Google Analytics is by far the most popular tool so I'll be using it to give examples, but the same principles can be applied to almost all web analytics tools. Google Analytics is also free (it has a premium version, but you should start with the free one), so I suggest you create an account to get the feel of it.

If you don't have a website or data yet, Google Analytics provides a demo account that you can use.

Let's start with some definitions. A metric is all the things that you can count on your website, like users, conversions, revenue and sessions.

Usually, you will use dimensions to analyze and break down your data. A dimension is anything that cannot be counted, such as country, device, gender etc. For example, if you'd like to see where your users come from you'd select the metric users and break it down by the dimension country.

Web analytics tools have dozens of metrics and dimensions you can use, but don't be intimidated. Instead, focus on the few metrics that really matter to your business. How many users visited your website? How many of them bought something or sigend up for a newsletter? Which pages get the most traffic?

Next use dimensions to slice your data, dig deeper into your reports and answer business questions. For example, you might observe that desktop has a much higher conversion rate than mobile. Is that because people tend to buy things on desktop or does the mobile version of your website have a technical problem? You could investigate further by looking into different browsers and see if they show big differences in conversion rates. That might mean that your site doesn't render well on a particular browser.

You could also monitor your best-performing campaigns by breaking down your campaigns by conversion rate, or find out when people visit your website by creating a report with the metric sessions and the dimension Day of Week or Hour of Day.

Country	Acquisition	
	Users ? ↓	
	14,547 % of Total: 100.00% (14,547)	
1. United States	**5,969**	(41.37%)
2. India	**1,048**	(7.26%)
3. United Kingdom	**850**	(5.89%)
4. Canada	**497**	(3.44%)
5. Germany	**365**	(2.53%)
6. France	**323**	(2.24%)
7. Taiwan	**323**	(2.24%)
8. Japan	**289**	(2.00%)
9. Spain	**287**	(1.99%)
10. South Korea	**282**	(1.95%)

A Google Analytics report that shows how many users visit the website from each country.

So how do you get started with Google Analytics or any other web analytics tool? The first thing you have to do is to install a piece of code on your website.

As soon as you do that the tool will start collecting data and generating reports. The tool will track all the visits but if you'd like to track certain actions, e.g. someone pressing a button, downloading an e-book, signing up for a newletter or buying something, you'll have to set up what is known as goals.

Goals should essentially align with your business goals so you can track the performance of your website and marketing activities. Analytics is an essential tool for monitoring and optimizing the performance of your website and digital marketing.

Without data you're in the dark so better set up that analytics tool sooner rather than later.

Put analytics in the core of
your business

Analytics can be instrumental for your success in the online world. Without measuring you can't make proper decisions and analytics can reveal the pain points and successes of your business.

Analytics will also show you how people behave on the web when they interact with your company, from the first time they see an ad from you to their first visit to your website and even when they make a purchase.

Let's say you have a barber shop and use your website for reservations among other things. That is your main goal that you'd like your users to complete when they visit your website, as it means more business for your barber shop.

Using analytics you can see how many reservations for a haircut were made but also all the actions that led to the reservation (also known as customer journey).

Let's put ourselves in the user's shoes for a moment. Imagine you want to get a haircut in a new area you just moved to. You search for "barber shops in my area" on Google and visit a few websites comparing their prices, the pictures and videos they feature and other info you might be interested in.

While on the webstie you"ll probably check the price list, see some testimonials, read the blog if the site has one etc. You're not booking the reservation yet because you still have time and you want to think about it. You want to look slick after all! But you do have a few favorites based on the criteria you think are important.

So you decide to sign up for the newsletter of our example's barber shop since it say on the homepage that they regularly give offers to their newsletter readers.

A few days later you receive a 20% off coupon for a haircut in your email inbox. Right before that party you're planning to attend and want to look your best.

You've already compared different barber shops in your area and had 2-3 on your shortlist so this email is a great incentive for you to make your final decision. You click on the offer listed in the email, go to the website and reserve a spot for a haircut.

Analytics can reveal all the actions that the users took to finally make a reservation. You see how many people found out about your barber shop through online search, how many people signed up for your newsletter and how many reservations were made.

You can see info on which channels were the most efficient for sending people to your website or generating reservations for your barber shop.

A goal funnel in Google Analytics.

You can see what people did on your website once they were sent there by a search engine, display ad or a social network. Which pages did they visit? Did they watch a video before signing up for a newsletter? Or did they book a reservation right away?

Analytics can help you monitor your goals, like reservations in our example. Moreover, you can see if people come back to your website and if they become loyal customers.

A goal doesn't have to be a monetary transaction (e.g. a purchase) but it can include all kinds of things someone can do on your website and you think are important, such as watching a video, reading a blog article, signing up for a newsletter or downloading a free e-book.

And of course any step in the purchase funnel must be tracked properly to monitor potential drop-offs. For example, a typical purchase funnel for an e-store consists of the following steps: View Product > Add to Cart > Start Checkout > Add Payment Details > Complete Purchase.

You might notice that there is a large drop-off after the "Add Payment Details" step. Maybe you're making this form really long and cumbersome for your users resulting in them abandoning the checkout process. Or you might find out that by retargeting people who added items to their cart but left (e.g. by following up with an email offering a 10% discount) you get them to finally purchase your products.

Analytics can and should be in the core of your business so that you make better decisions and optimize your online strategy.

Track goals and conversions

To better utilize your data you eed to make sure that you're monitoring the goals you have as a business.

Thus, every company should have a different analytics setup based on the goals and conversions that they'd like to track.

Conversions in analytics and digital marketing parlance is when a user completes one of the goals that you've set. Let's use a restaurant that takes online reservations as an example.

As teh restaurant owner you check your analytics reports and see that your website had a 50% increase in traffic this month compared to last month. At first you're excited, but this number doesn't really mean anything on its own. Traffic is a nice thing to have but unless it leads to conversions it's meaningless.

So, you try to find out if all this traffic you get has any value. You notice that your visitors spend an average of three minutes on your website, not really different from the behavior they exhibited in the previous months.

One thing to keep in mind that metrics need context to be evaluated. Is three minutes a long time to spend on your site? Do those three minutes lead to a conversion? We don't really know just by looking at this metric. We need to look into other metrics to come to a conclusion.

Those metric should be the ones that reflect the reasons that your business is online. You first created a website in order to increase your reservations by having people book a table online. You have a form on a website that peopel use to make reservations. This is the primary goal you track on your website but there are also other secondary goals that you monitor.

For example, people signing up for a newsletter means that people want to hear from you or are interested in special offers.

What else did you set up the webstite for? Well, you wanted to give website visitors more information about your restaurant. For example, your contact details page is one of the things that you want people to know. So, all the visits to the page that includes your address, phone and map is a goal that can be tracked as it shows that people are interested in your restaurant.

When it comes to your business think about all the actions on your website that have a value. That's not limited to monetary value, i.e. purchases; anythign that can lead to a user moving further down into the marketing funnel could be a goal.

All these goals should be set up in your web analytics tool and monitored in the corresponding reports and dashboards.

	Goal	↓	Id	Goal Type
☐	Engaged Users		Goal ID 2 / Goal Set 1	Pages/Screens per session
☐	Entered Checkout		Goal ID 4 / Goal Set 1	Destination
☐	Purchase Completed		Goal ID 1 / Goal Set 1	Destination
☐	Registrations		Goal ID 3 / Goal Set 1	Destination
☐	Smart Goals		Goal ID 5 / Goal Set 1	Smart Goal

You can add up to 20 goals in Google Analytics.

Now your reports become much clearer and insightful. Instead of, say, looking just at the number of visitors you get, you can see what percentage of visitors convert (complete one of your goals). And you can break this down by various dimensions such as acquisition channel, location, browser, device etc.

Let's say you see that people tend to make more reservations on weekends. So, what action do you take? You could, for example, run more ads on weekends to maximize their conversion rate. Or send special offers for weekdays only in your newsletter to make sure that you don't have a full restaurant on weekends only.

These are just examples of how you can use web analytics to make better decisions and optimize your marketing activities. By tracking the things that matter to yor business you can take meaningful actions and improve your company's online performance.

Measure organic search

One of the most important traffic sources is visits that come from search engines. Web analytics tools can help you find out if your search traffic is increasing or decreasing, what people do on your webstie after they find it on a search engine, and how you can optimize your website to ensure that people who find you on search results are actually interested in your products.

Source	Acquisition			Behavior	
	Users ↓	New Users	Sessions	Bounce Rate	Pages / Session
	8,048 % of Total: 58.65% (13,723)	**6,862** % of Total: 58.47% (11,735)	**9,278** % of Total: 55.84% (16,616)	**53.72%** Avg for View: 45.85% (17.17%)	**3.39** Avg for View: 3.98 (-14.74%)
1. google	**7,667** (95.56%)	**6,526** (95.10%)	**8,897** (95.89%)	52.87%	3.46
2. baidu	**253** (3.15%)	**248** (3.61%)	**255** (2.75%)	85.88%	1.25
3. bing	**67** (0.84%)	**54** (0.79%)	**84** (0.91%)	45.24%	2.94
4. duckduckgo	**15** (0.19%)	**15** (0.22%)	**19** (0.20%)	47.37%	3.26
5. yahoo	**13** (0.16%)	**11** (0.16%)	**15** (0.16%)	46.67%	2.40
6. yandex	**7** (0.09%)	**7** (0.10%)	**7** (0.08%)	85.71%	1.14
7. ask	**1** (0.01%)	**1** (0.01%)	**1** (0.01%)	100.00%	1.00

In Google Analytics you can see the different engines that people use to visit your site.

You can monitor how many users come to your website from different search engines and it's a good idea to track their trends over time.

Digging deeper, you'll want to see the keywords that people use on search engines to end up on your website. Usually to get this data on Google Analytics you'll have to integrate it with Google Search Console. This is pretty straightforward and it's worth it as you'll get valuable insights on what people search for. This can be a great insight for your paid search campaigns. Even if you're not running any paid search now, when you decide to do it you'll have a great starting point on which keywords to use.

Moreover, you can improve your website to match your visitors' searches. For example, you might find out that the visitors to your barber shop website regularly search for the term "Brad Pitt new haircut". You might want to consider including a blog post on how to style your hair like Brad Pitt and you might even tout the fact that you indeed specialize in this type of haircut.

Keyword	Acquisition			Behavior
	Users ↓	New Users	Sessions	Bounce Rate
	87 % of Total: 0.63% (13,723)	77 % of Total: 0.66% (11,735)	105 % of Total: 0.63% (16,616)	54.29% Avg for View: 45.85% (18.41%)
1. google merchandise store	22 (23.91%)	19 (24.68%)	26 (24.76%)	53.85%
2. google merchandise	5 (5.43%)	4 (5.19%)	5 (4.76%)	60.00%
3. google store	3 (3.26%)	2 (2.60%)	3 (2.86%)	100.00%
4. youtube merch	3 (3.26%)	2 (2.60%)	4 (3.81%)	25.00%
5. google apparel	2 (2.17%)	2 (2.60%)	2 (1.90%)	50.00%
6. google merch	2 (2.17%)	1 (1.30%)	2 (1.90%)	50.00%
7. google merchandise shop	2 (2.17%)	2 (2.60%)	2 (1.90%)	50.00%
8. Google Merchandise Store	2 (2.17%)	0 (0.00%)	3 (2.86%)	0.00%
9. google official merchandise store	2 (2.17%)	1 (1.30%)	2 (1.90%)	50.00%
10. google shirt	2 (2.17%)	1 (1.30%)	2 (1.90%)	50.00%

A list of keywords from organic search on Google Analytics.

Add more content that is relevant to the most frequently searched keywords and keep an eye on the latest trends on your visitors' keyword searches to update your blog and videos accordingly.

Moreover, you can see what actions ceratin keywords lead to. For example, people from a popular might come to your website and read your content but not really make reservations; whereas less popular keywords might lead to actual bookings and other types of conversions. So, remember what we said in the previous chapter: analytics are meaningful when you look into the metrics that matter, i.e. your goals.

After you've improved your website by updating the content based on the analytics data you'll have to verify that your hard work paid off. Make sure to monitor the performance of the new content and pages and see if it actually made a difference to the conversion rate of those specific pages and your website as a whole.

Measure paid search

Measuring your paid marketing activities is even more important than measuring organic traffic, because you're spending money to run your ads. It's crucial that you understand how your campaigns perform and how you can optimize them to get a positive return on investment.

Let's revisit our beaty salon example. Let's say you offer different beauty and makeup packages that people can book online on your website. You run different paid search campaigns for bridal makeup, facial cleanings, massage etc.

You'd like to know which of these campaigns are profitable. You look at your analytics report for paid search campaigns and you realize that for the "Wedding makeup" campaign you have an overall 6% conversion rate, i.e. for every 100 visitors that this campaign brings to the website 6 go on to book a makeup session. You break down the campaign by keyword and see that the keyword "bridal makeup" have a 7% conversion rate whereas the keyword "wedding beauty prep" has a 1% conversion rate and a much higher CPC (cost per click). Clearly, you cna invest more money on the fromer keyword and probably pause the latter, if it's cost exceeds the money it brings in.

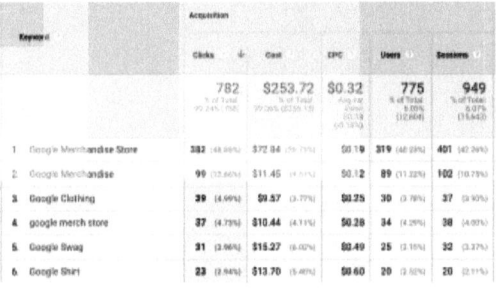

Google Analytics can show you a slew of metrics on your Google Ads keywords and content.

You can also use this insight to improve the campaign by looking at the relevant content on your page and see if you could make changes by using the best-performing keywords and testing different messages to see which one resonates more with your audience.

You should also test and monitor the ad content you're running for your search campaigns. Your "Wedding makeup" campaign might have two ads: ad A has the headline "Best wedding makeup" and ad B says "Bridal makeup - special offer".

This can show you which ad content has the best performance with your audience and you should be trying out different messages, keywords and content to optimize your campaigns.

If you're using Google Analytics make sure you connect it with your Google Ads account so that it automatically imports all your campaign data for you and you can monitor your Google Paid Search activity.

You can also use the data to adjust your bids and get the most of out them. Keep an eye on the price you pay for every click and adjust your bid to see which bid level had the best conversion rate. You might find out that by bidding a bit lower or higher you might improve your overall results.

At the end of the day you want to make sure that the budget you're spending on search ads brings back a profit, and analytics is the best way to ensure your success.

Segmentation

Segmentation is the act of breaking down data to get deeper insights.

For example, using the beauty salon example, you see that the overall conversion rate for your website is 4%. You decide to delve deeper into the data and break down all the website users by location. People who, let's say, live in the north part of your region have an 8% conversion rate whereas other areas bring in a lot of traffic but their conversion rate is low.

You decide to direct more local ads to the north part of your region as it seems to convert better, while trying to customize some of your content to cater to other areas and see if their conversion rate improves.

Next, you can break down visitors by their age group. You might find out that you get conversions from a wide range of ages, but women in the 35-45 age group tend to spend more money and make repeat bookings. As a business you can decide if you want to focus your content on that age group; or maybe you can try and work toward convincing the rest of the age groups to become repeat customers.

Let's now break down traffic by their device type.

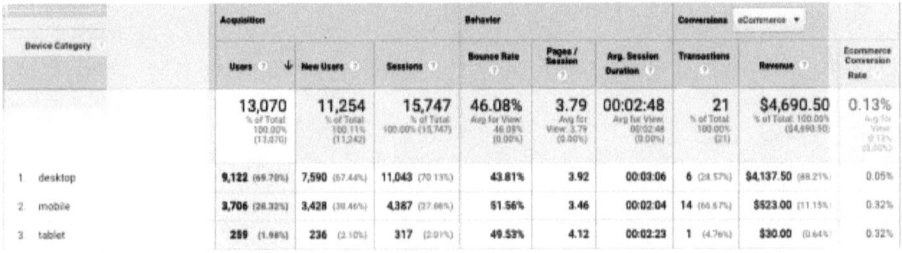

A Google Analytics breakdown of different device types.

You might see that both desktop and mobile bring in considerable traffic. However, desktop has a much higher conversion rate than mobile. Is it because your mobile website experience is not as effective as the desktop one? You could break down further by browser and specific device brands to see if your site does not render properly on specific browsers.

Or could it be just the fact that your audience prefers to use their desktop computer? Segmentation often sheds a light on the data but you'll have to use your knowledge about your business to make the final decision and find out how to optimize your company's performance.

After all, nobody knows your business as well as you do! Now go and break down the data of your website. You can apply multiple breakdowns, for example segment your audience by country and then by age group and gender.

This is the detective work that web analysts do to uncover the clues about online performance.

Know your audience

The data you gather from analytics can help you understand your users in order to optimize your business performance.

First, you have all the quantitative data which you can access through your analytics tool: how many people visited the site, how many conversions they did etc.

On top of that you could try and obtain qualitative data, such as people's opinions about your products or your brand.

Usually a combination of the two types of data will give you a better picture of your audience. Your quantitative data is already available through your analytics tool; in order to get qualitative data you need to get people's input, by having them fill in a survey, getting their reviews on your website or just asking them directly.

You can also combine online and offline sources. For example, the results of a poll on Facebook about your product can be complemented by a survey that customers take at your physical store.

For your own business, think about the sources of qualitative and quantitative data and how you can use them to understand your audience and make better decisions.

From data to insights

Analytics tools can offer a wealth of data, but the real value appears when you turn data into insights that help you make better decisions.

To put it simply, data shows what happened: how many people visited your website or how much revenue you generated from their visits. Insights refers to why it happened: why do people in certain locations buy more of your products, why some campaigns perform better than others etc.

Actionable insights are insights that can be used to make decisions in order to improve your company's performance.

In order to unearth actionable insights you'll usually follow the steps below:

- Define your business goals: Your analytics and data should exist to serve the business goals of your company

- Collect the data relevant to your goals: You'll have a ton of data for many different metrics, but focus on the ones that matter to your business

- Analyze the data: Identify trends, patterns and outliers when you break down the data

- Turn data into insights and hypotheses: Based on the analysis you did, come up with suggestions and recommendations on how to improve your performance

- Test your hypotheses: Put your money where your mouth is and implement your suggestions

- Evaluate: Did your recommendations actually improve business results based on your goals?

Remember that this process is iterative. Data and insights

change, and so should your hypotheses. You should frequently update your findings and test your new hypotheses.

The only way to know if something's working is to test and evaluate it.

Let's see an example. Imagine you're organizing a concert with local bands. You need to get at least five thousand people to buy tickets from your website to be profitable.

Ticket purchases are obviously your primary goal on your website so you gather the data from your analytics tool and break it down to see which channels bring in most of the conversions.

It seems that Facebook and Instagram are doing a great job of convincing people to buy a ticket, but you want to delve deeper and see what kind of posts perform the best.

Your reports suggest that videos with local bands advertising the event have the highest conversion rates. So, your recommendation is to produce more of those videos with bands that you haven't yet posted on your Facebook page.

Your plan is to make those videos, post them and measure the results and see if your overall conversion rate increases.

This process of gathering data, turning them into insights, testing them and evaluating them should guide your overall marketing and business activity. Focus only on the data that is relevant to your business and its goals and try to review the trends for those goals. It helps if you set up some reports and dashboards for the metrics that matter to your business and review them on a daily, weekly and monthly basis.

Check the timeline and overall trends and if there are any outliers and anomalies in the data. Next, think of how you can apply the findings to improve your decisions. Test your hypotheses and assess them and then go back to get more insights and further improve your performance.

E-COMMERCE

Set up your e-shop

Even if your company sells its products in a physical store it's always a good idea to expand your sales by offering the option of online purchases to your audience.

Your e-store can have multiple functions like searching for various products and seeing if they are available in inventory, accepting payments and creating customer accounts.

In order to be able to sell online you need to set up a store with your products and the ability to accept payments via services like PayPal. The easiest way to set up an e-shop is by using a platform like Shopify or Squarespace.

These ecom platforms allow you to create a website without having to know how to code. They have a wealth of templates that you can use and offer integrations with payment systems and other services.

Make sure to include high-quality photos and detailed descriptions of your product. Reviews from people who bought the item can also give more information to potential customers.

Often the difference between products that sell well and those who don't is the wealth of information (in video, image and text) that you provide to the user. Your products should also be easily searcheable and places under categories so it's easier for the website visitors to find what they're looking for.

If you don't want to jump straight ahead into creating your own e-shop, you can alwats use marketplaces like Amazon and eBay. The advantage is that you don't have to set up a store on your website and you're selling on a platform used and trusted by millions. The downsides are that you'll have to pay a commission for every sale you make and you're competing against other companies selling similar products on the marketplace.

An important part of your online shop is managing payments and orders. Services like PayPal or Stripe enable you to accept payments through credit or debit cards or online accounts.

Usually, those third-party payment services will let you add a button to your website which users click when they want to purchase something. This will lead them to a form they have to complete to make the payment. That form usually lives on the third-party website and when it's complete the users is directed back to your website where they will see a confirmation of their order.

Online payment services will charge you a fee for every transaction, usually a small percentage of the total value. They will handle all the payments for you and are trusted both by merchants and consumers, letting you focus on optimizing your store and business.

Ecom services like Shopify and Magento feature an order backend system that enables customers to create accounts with their personal information, shipping addresses and billing information. This is really helpful if you have repeat customers so that they don't have to fill in the same info over and over every time they make a purchase.

What's more, you can use the info on the backend system to reward your loyal customers, send them offers and make the overall experience more convenient and pleasant for them.

Moreover, many of the ecom services offer solutions like shipping tracking, integration with several systems like accounting, linking directly to wholesale merchants etc.

Using an off-the-shelf solution can save you time and effort for a small monthly sum, so that you can focus on activities like marketing and business strategy to make the most out of your online presence.

Optimize your e-com experience

The first thing you want to get absolutely right about your e-store is that people experience a smooth purchase process on all devices. Imagine if a customer really wants to buy something from your e-shop but your mobile website keeps breaking down. Not only you've lost a customer, but you've also made a disappointing impression that will likely impact your company image.

A good way to start is by looking at your analytics data and break down your visits and purchases by device. If you notice that people on mobile visit your website but don't really make a purchase, something's wrong. Maybe users are not able to see your products properly, the website is too slow or there might be a problem with payments on mobile devices.

Looking at your customer journey step by step (e.g. website visit > product view > add to cart > initiate checkout > payment details > purchase completed) is a good way to understand where the problem lies in. Remember to break down by dimensions like device, operation system, browser, language, location etc.

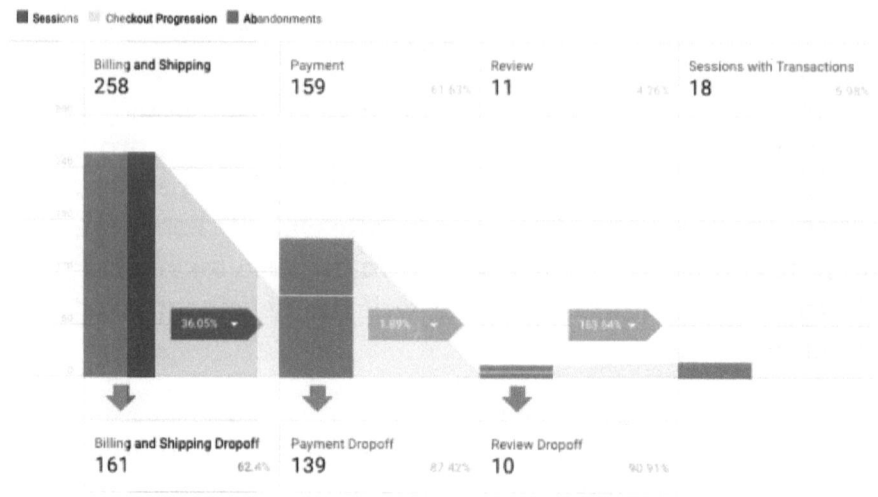

Analytics tools can help you understand where dropoffs happen during the shopping and checkout process.

As we've noted before your website design should be responsive, i.e. it should adapt to different devices and screen sizes.

However, let's say you find out that people on all devices come to your website but don't really buy your products. Then you'll have to think about how easy it is for people to find what they're looking for. Is there a search function they can use? Are the products organized in categories and subcategories?

A good idea is to A/B test different layouts and structures for your website and if you can, also gather feedback from users on their experience. You'll be surprised by how different their experience to your website is. For you everything seems easy because you've seen the website thousands of times and you know every little bit of it; but for a first time visitor the experience might be confusing and intimidating.

Another example is that people visit your product pages but they don't really add them to their cart. How can you convince them to do this? Remember that a product page should give as much information as possible without becoming overwhelming. Are there quality pictures of the product from different angles? How about a video? Have you included a great description with all the features of the product? Often, users want to also see reviews from other people who bought the product to know what they think about it.

If you notice that the steepest drop-off for people happens at the last step of the purchase process, you might want to encourage users to open an account and store their shipping and billing information. Next time they will come to your site their info will be saved so they just have to press a button to complete the purchase.

Moreover, you can use people's past orders to personalize their experience by recommending similar products or by up-selling and cross-selling. You can also use customer data to reward repeat customers with loyalty points, spceial offers and discounts.

All in all, look at your data, identify the pain points, improve the experience and make your customers feel valued.

Make people come back to your e-shop

You've all probably visited a website, viewed a product and added it to cart but didn't end up buying it. You've also noticed that right after this you started seeing ads for that product or similar products on social media and other websites.

This is thanks to retargeting a form of advertising that we've seen before, where you can specifically target people who've already visited your website or have taken a specific action.

The fact that someone views a product or adds it to cart reveals a lot about their buying preferences and intent. This information can be used by your business to convince people to take the last step and buy the product they're interested in.

The way retargeting works is by placing a tracking code on your website. When a visitor comes to your website you can track what actions they took, such as adding a product to cart or purchasing something, as well as the products that people viewed.

No personally identifiable information is stored anywhere so you'll never know the name, email or other personal information about the customer. The tracking code just tracks what they did on the website.

Using this tracking code you can create audiences, e.g. all the people who added something to cart but didn't buy anything, people who visited your website in the past 30 days, people who are interested in product X etc.

Now you're ready to run retargeting campaigns using those audiences. So, when the user who added a product to cart leaves your website and visits some other website, e.g. a news website, a display ad showing that very product will appear.

If you feel that the customers who don't complete the purchase need an extra incentive to buy the product you can include a discount or special offer in your ad. Services like Google Ads and Criteo offer retargeting solutions such as the example above.

It's very simple to use these services and the first thing you need to do is place their tracking code on your website so that they can collect the data to target the specific audiences you're interested in.

After you've created those audiences and set up specific rules for retargeting, the service will start serving your ads to those people when they visit websites that are part of their huge network.

Moreover, your ads can be dynamic, as we like to call them. Let's explain this with an example. Amazon.com offers literally millions of products on their website and they retarget users after they've viewed a product. However, it would be impossible to create a different ad for each and every product or a separate audience for every product viewed. So how do they show the right ad to the right person every time?

This handled by the tracking code and retargeting service. Amazon.com just places the tracking code on all of its pages and creates a dynamic campaign for all the people who viewed a product or added it to their cart. The tracking code stores the product ID for every used who took this action, so when they show the user the ad they will show the same product as they viewed on Amazon.com. All Amazon needs to do is upload a file (also known as product catalog) with all their product IDs on the retargeting service and the service will match the user's info - taken from the tracking code - with the right ID on the catalog.

When running retargeting campaigns you should set rules to make sure you get the most out of them. For example, set a limit on how many times a user can see the ad and for how long. You don't want people seeing the ad for a really long amount of time as they might buy the product from somewhere else or just stop being interested in it, and you'll still be paying to deliver the ad to them.

Moreover, you don't have to always offer a discounted price when showing the retargeting ad. People might abandon the on-line shopping journey for several reasons and while a discount might be enticing to them, you might be reducing your profit margin for no reason.

As we've noted before the golden rule for any type of market-ing activity is to monitor your campaigns' performance and optimize accordingly. Make sure you measure the improtant metrics like conversion rates; run tests fro differnet ad formats, creatives and audiences; and set up reports to see if you're im-proving your performance over time.

Another way to make sure your website visitors are engaged and are getting a great experience is to promote the right prod-ucts on your homepage and landing pages.

While someone is browsing your store, data on their prefer-ences - such as products and categories - is collected. This data can be used to promote relevant products and predict what they might be interested in.

Ecom solutions like Shopify and Magento feature these prod-uct recommendation engines and personalize the shopping and browsing experience for your users.

This is also a great way to keep users coming back to your web-site since they know they will find something relevant to their interests. If you sell a wide array of products this method can help you cross-sell and up-sell and also build customer loyalty.

www.ingramcontent.com/pod-product-compliance
Lightning Source LLC
Chambersburg PA
CBHW030624220526
45463CB00004B/1403